EXPLRING

GERMAN

Second Edition

Joan G. Sheeran
J. Patrick McCarthy

Consultant
Wolfgang S. Kraft

EMC Publishing, Saint Paul, Minnesota

PROPERTY OF
No._____
HANOVER SCHOOL BOARD,

with special thanks to:
David and Leslie Neira—musical editing, general
  and photographic assistance
James Douglas Sheeran—editorial advice
Judy G. Myrth—reading, editing, suggestions and
  other assistance
Mary Jo Horan—artistic inspiration
Jackie Urbanovic—illustrations
The Nancekivell Group—cover design
*Paul Renslo, Eileen Slater and the students of Oak-
  Land Junior High School*—photographic
  assistance
Christine M. Gray—desktop production
Christine Gensmer—project management

photo credits:
Mike Woodside Photography—cover
NASA—Earth
Austrian National Tourist Office—p. vii (br)
German Information Center—p. xii (br)
Wolfgang S. Kraft—p. iii, p. vi (b), p. vii (bl),
  p. viii (all), p. ix (all), p. x (all), p. xi (all),
  p. xii (t, bl)
Swiss National Tourist Office—p. vi (t), p. vii (t)

ISBN 0-8219-1197-X

© 1995 by EMC Corporation

All rights reserved. No part of this publication may
be adapted, reproduced, stored in a retrieval
system or transmitted in any form or by any means
electronic, mechanical, photocopying, recording, or
otherwise without permission from the publisher.

Published by EMC Publishing
300 York Avenue
St. Paul, Minnesota 55101

Printed in the United States of America
1 2 3 4 5 6 7 8 9 10 XXX 99 98 97 96 95

INTRODUCTION

Hallo und willkommen!

Hello and welcome! Did you know that one out of every four Americans are of German ancestry? Even if you aren't from a German background, you are probably curious about exploring a world where over 100 million people communicate in German every day. Many of these German speakers deal with Americans, since Germany is the United States' largest trading partner in Europe. In *Exploring German* you will learn some common words and expressions that these people use daily. If you learn these basic words and expressions, and if you have the opportunity to travel to one of the European countries where people speak German, you will be able to understand some of the things they say. They will also be able to understand you. As the world continues to shrink and as countries and people grow closer and closer together, it is important to be able to communicate with each other.

If you practice correct pronunciation with your teacher or with the audiocassettes, you will learn to speak German even better. Besides being able to understand and speak basic German, you will find out some information about Germany and get some insight into the country's rich traditions in art, music and literature. Hopefully, throughout your journey you will discover that learning German is fun and not too difficult. Be sure to practice your German at every opportunity both in and outside of class. As with any other skill, the more you practice, the better you will become.

So, let's get started! *Also, los!*

Table of Contents

Exploring

...countries and cities

Valser Valley, Switzerland

Rhine River, Germany

Zurich, Switzerland

Vienna, Austria

Frankfurt, Germany

Germany

Germany

Zell, Germany

Germany

Eutin, Germany

...daily life

Frankfurt, Germany

Germany

Berlin, Germany

Osnabrück, Germany

Germany

Osnabrück, Germany

Neuschwanstein Castle, Germany

Linderhof Castle, Germany

Munich, Germany

GREETINGS AND COURTESY
Begrüßungen und Höflichkeit

Guten Morgen.
Good Morning.
Guten Tag.
Hello.
Guten Abend.
Good Evening.
Gute Nacht.
Good Night.

Höflichkeit

Bitte. ———— Please.
Danke. ———— Thank you.
Bitte (schön). — You're welcome.
Entschuldigung. — Excuse me.
Es tut mir leid. – I'm sorry.

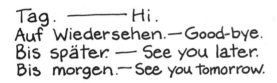

Tag. ——— Hi.
Auf Wiedersehen. — Good-bye.
Bis später. — See you later.
Bis morgen. — See you tomorrow.

Ja.

Nein.

Viel Glück.

GOOD LUCK!

Wie heißt du?
What's your name?

Ich heiße Josef.
My name is Josef.

Du sprichst deutsch, nicht wahr?
You speak German, don't you?

Ja. Ich spreche deutsch.
Yes. I speak German.

Angenehm.
Es freut mich.
I'm pleased to meet you.

Wie geht's?
How are you?

Gut, danke,
Und dir?
Fine thanks. And you?

Nicht schlecht.
Not bad.

Sprichst du deutsch?
Do you speak German?

Nein. Ich spreche nicht deutsch.
No. I don't speak German.

Tschüß = So long.   Spanisch (Spanish), Französisch (French),
Englisch (English), Italienisch (Italian), Russisch (Russian)

Höflichkeit ist Trumpf.   Courtesy is power.

Ich heiße...

Antje	Andreas
Bettina	Dieter
Brigitte	Erich
Christl	Franz
Erika	Fritz
Evelyn	Günter
Gisela	Heinz
Heidi	Holger
Julia	Hans
Jutta	Josef
Karin	Kurt
Luise	Lars
Maria	Manfred
Marianne	Michael
Martina	Patrick
Monika	Robert
Renate	Rudolf
Rita	Stefan
Sabine	Werner
Susanne	Willi

Exercises

A Wähle das nicht zutreffende Wort! *Choose the word which does not fit.*

1. Nacht	Morgen	Tag	Glück
2. deutsch	nein	englisch	französisch
3. Angenehm.	Bis später.	Tschüß.	Auf Wiedersehen.
4. Bitte.	Danke.	Bitte sehr.	Ja.
5. Wie heißt du?	Wie geht's?	Nicht wahr?	Sprichst du spanisch?

B Wähle nur Mädchennamen. *Choose only girls' names.*

1. Gisela	6. Christl
2. Heinz	7. Werner
3. Günter	8. Dieter
4. Bettina	9. Luise
5. Sabine	10. Andreas

C Beantworte die Fragen auf deutsch! Schreib deine Antworten! *Answer the questions in German. Write your answers.*

1. Wie geht's? _____

2. Sprichst du deutsch? _____

3. Wie heißt du? _____

D Schreib zu jeder Abbildung einen Ausdruck auf deutsch! *Write in German an expression that corresponds to each illustration.*

1. _____

2. _____

3. _____

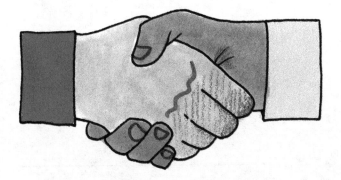

4. _____

5. _____

6. _____

7. _____

E Short Answers (Auf deutsch, bitte.).

1. How do you wish someone "good luck"?

   _____

2. *"Tag"* is a short version of

   _____

3. How do you greet someone in the morning?

   _____

4. How do you greet someone in the evening?

   _____

5. How do you say "good-bye"?

   _____

6. *"Nein"* is the opposite of

   _____

7. An expression at an introduction is

   _____

8. Answer this question: *"Wie geht's?"*

   _____

9. Do German speakers tend to shake hands more frequently than Americans?

   _____

10. "Please" means _____

F Beantworte die Fragen auf deutsch! *Answer the questions in German.* Schreib deine Antworten. *Write your answers.*

1. Werner: Guten Morgen, Angelika. Wie geht's?

   Angelika: _____

2. Heidi: Sprichst du englisch, Markus?

   Markus: _____

3. Günter: Tag! Ich heiße Günter. Wie heißt du?

   Luise: _____

Kreuzworträtsel

G

Vertical

1. opposite of "ja"
2. "Du sprichst deutsch, nicht . . . ?"
4. expected response to a favor
6. sometimes needed at exam time
7. opposite of "Nacht"
8. "Ich . . . (My name is)" Note: ß = ss
10. ". . . geht's?"
11. "Ich . . . deutsch."
12. "Abend" auf englisch
16. "Wie heißt . . . ?"

Horizontal

3. normal evening greeting
5. opposite of "Tag"
6. opposite of "schlecht"
9. said when departing
13. German word for "I"
14. ". . . Glück."
15. courteous request
17. spoken in Austria, Switzerland and Germany
18. part of the day in which school begins

Herzlich willkommen!

Herzliche
Weihnachtsgrüße
und alles Gute im
Neuen Jahr

Zum Einzug ins neue Heim
viel Glück!

GRUSS AUS HAMBURG

Herzlichen
Glückwunsch
zum
Geburtstag

CLASSROOM OBJECTS
Die Klasse

2

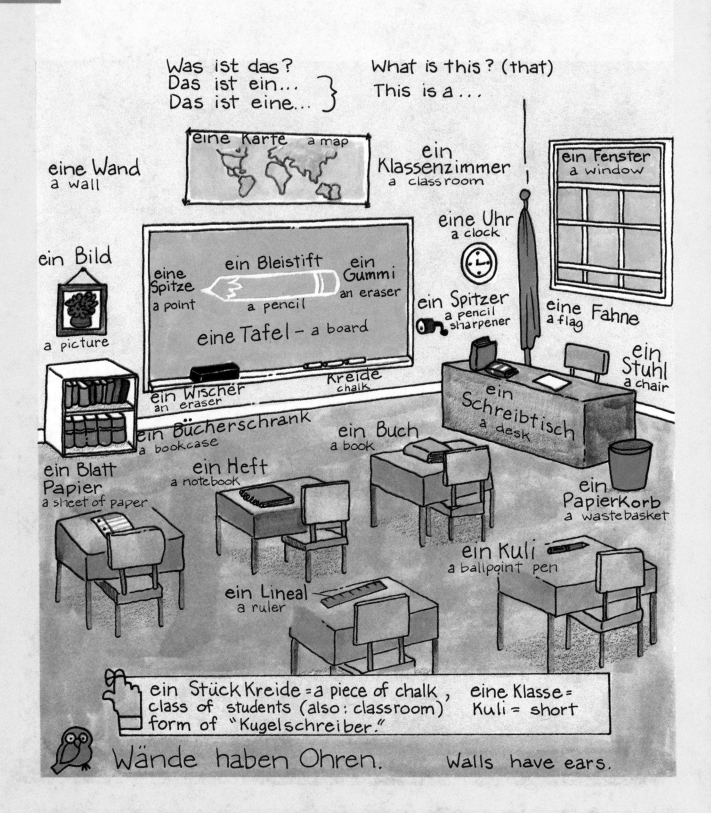

Was ist das?
Das ist ein...
Das ist eine... }

What is this? (that)
This is a...

eine Karte — a map

eine Wand — a wall

ein Klassenzimmer — a classroom

ein Fenster — a window

ein Bild — a picture

eine Spitze — a point

ein Bleistift

ein Gummi — an eraser

a pencil

eine Uhr — a clock

ein Spitzer — a pencil sharpener

eine Fahne — a flag

ein Stuhl — a chair

eine Tafel — a board

ein Wischer — an eraser

Kreide — chalk

ein Bücherschrank — a bookcase

ein Schreibtisch — a desk

ein Buch — a book

ein Papierkorb — a wastebasket

ein Blatt Papier — a sheet of paper

ein Heft — a notebook

ein Kuli — a ballpoint pen

ein Lineal — a ruler

ein Stück Kreide = a piece of chalk , eine Klasse = class of students (also: classroom) Kuli = short form of "Kugelschreiber."

Wände haben Ohren.   Walls have ears.

Exercises

A Your teacher will point out 24 classroom objects. As your teacher pronounces each object in German, find it on the list below and place the appropriate number after it.

eine Spitze _____

ein Stuhl _____

ein Kuli _____

ein Lineal _____

ein Blatt Papier _____

eine Karte _____

ein Klassenzimmer _____

ein Wischer _____

eine Klasse

ein Gummi _____

ein Buch _____

ein Papierkorb _____

ein Stück Kreide _____

ein Fenster _____

eine Wand _____

ein Schreibtisch _____

ein Heft _____

eine Uhr _____

ein Spitzer _____

ein Bild _____

eine Fahne _____

ein Bücherschrank _____

eine Tafel _____

ein Bleistift _____

B Answer each question in English.

1. Where in the classroom is the "Fahne"?

   _____

2. How many "Fenster" are in this room?

   _____

3. What is the color of the "Tafel"?

   _____

4. Is the "Klassenzimmer" big or little?

   _____

5. What is kept in a "Bücherschrank"?

   _____

C Wähle die richtige Antwort! *Choose the correct response.*

1. Ink is used in a . . .
   a. Kuli   b. Bleistift
2. One sits on a . . .
   a. Stuhl   b. Schreibtisch
3. In order to write on the board one needs some . . .
   a. Kreide   b. Wand
4. Minutes and hours are indicated by the . . .
   a. Papierkorb   b. Uhr
5. A student writes assignments in a . . .
   a. Heft   b. Bleistift
6. In order to draw a straight line one uses a . . .
   a. Wischer   b. Lineal

D Schreib den deutschen Namen von jedem Objekt! *Write the German name of each object.*

1. _____

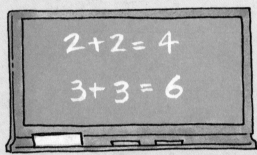

2. _____

3. _____

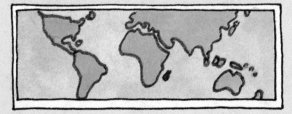

4. _____

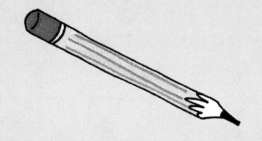

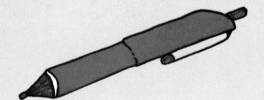

5. _____

6. _____

7. _____

8. _____

9. _____

10. _____

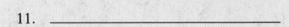

11. _____

12. _____

13. _____

14.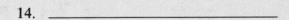

15. _____

E Ergänze die Sätze! *Complete the sentences.*

1. _____ ist das?

2. Das _____ ein Kuli.

3. Das ist _____ Fahne.

4. Das ist _____ Buch.

F Ergänze die fehlenden Buchstaben! *Complete the missing letters.*

1. Tafe___	9. Fe___ster	17. G___mmi
2. B___ld	10. Kart___	18. Bu___h
3. Wa___d	11. L___neal	19. Wi___cher
4. ___reide	12. S___itzer	20. Pap___er
5. Schrei___tisch	13. U___r	21. Klassen___immer
6. ___leistift	14. Fa___ne	22. Bücherschran___
7. Stuh___	15. Kul___	23. K___asse
8. Papierk___rb	16. ___eft	24. Sp___tze

Kreuzworträtsel

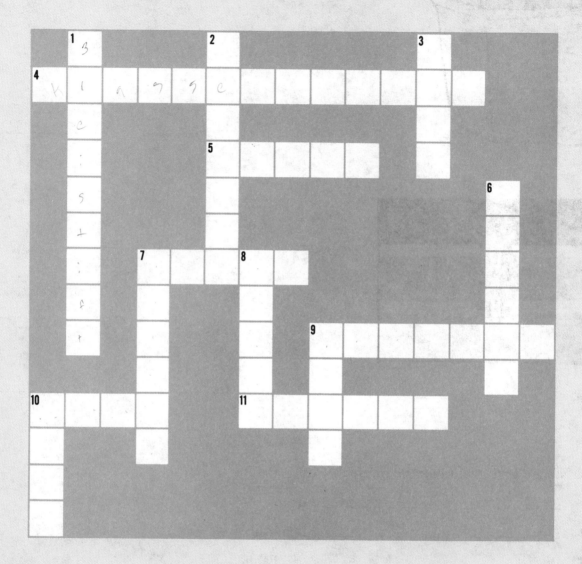

G

Vertical

1. writing instrument
2. where light is admitted
3. contains notes and assignments
6. lined or plain
7. white writing instrument
8. used with chalk
9. side of a room
10. source of information

Horizontal

4. place for instruction
5. place to sit
7. representation of geographical areas
9. used to erase the board
10. wall decoration
11. straight edge

Schulen und Hochschulen:

19 Grundschulen	Schüler	4 392
3 Hauptschulen	Schüler	530
6 Orientierungsstufen	Schüler	1 790
3 Realschulen	Schüler	996
5 Gymnasien	Schüler	4 003
2 Gesamtschulen	Schüler	2 089
1 Freie Waldorfschule	Schüler	410
3 Sonderschulen	Schüler	358
1 Abendgymnasium	Schüler	118
41 berufsbildende Schulen	Schüler	7 661
Georg-August-Universität	Studenten	31 404

ZEIT	MONTAG	DIENSTAG	MITTWOCH	DONNERSTAG	FREITAG	SAMSTAG
8⁰⁰ – 8⁴⁵	Deutsch	Biologie	Deutsch	Geschichte	Erdkunde	Mathe
8⁵⁰ – 9³⁵	Deutsch	Chemie	Mathe	Geschichte	Musik	Deutsch
9³⁵ – 9⁵⁰	Große Pause					Schwimmen
9⁵⁰ – 10³⁵	Englisch	Sport	Erdkunde	Physik	Deutsch	Schwimmen
10⁴⁰ – 11²⁵	Biologie	frei	Englisch	Französisch	Erdkunde	
11²⁵ – 11⁴⁰	Große Pause					
11⁴⁰ – 12²⁵	Französisch	Mathe	Französisch	Englisch	Englisch	
		Erdkunde	Kunst	Chemie	Französisch	

Nr. 0014

8 | 2 × 10 Filzschreiber **18⁹⁵**

9 | Sichthüllen **16⁹⁰**

10 | 5 Packbandrollen oder 10 Klebebandrollen **je 12⁹⁰**

Sichthüllen DIN A

15 | Rechner in Computerform **18⁹⁵**

11 | Maxi-Butler **29⁹⁵** Ohne Schreibutensilien

12
3 Notizblock-Würfel
15.-

PREIS-TIP

17 | Utensilien-Karussell
mit Inhalt **19⁹⁵**

Wiederhole!
Repeat.

Ergänze die Sätze!
Complete the sentences.

Sprich!
Speak.

Beantworte die Frage!
Answer the question.

Sag das auf deutsch!
Say that in German.

Heb die Hand!
Raise your hand.

Nimm Papier heraus.
Take out paper.

Mach das Buch auf!
Open the book.

Mach das Buch zu!
Close the book.

Schreib!
Write.

Hör zu!
Listen.

Lies!
Read.

Setz dich!
Sit down.

Ergänze die Sätze!
Complete the sentences.

Geh an die Tafel!
Go to the board.

 Was Hänschen nicht lernt, lernt Hans nimmermehr.

As the twig is bent, so grows the tree.

Exercises

A   Do what your teacher commands.

B   Schreib auf deutsch, bitte! *Write in German, please.*

1. (Speak.) _____

2. (Say.) _____

3. (Complete.) _____

C   Do what the following command orders you to do.

Schreib deinen Namen! _____

D   Was paßt zusammen? *What matches?*

A		**B**
1. schreiben	_____	a. to repeat
2. gehen	_____	b. to write
3. lesen	_____	c. to lift, raise
4. wiederholen	_____	d. to read
5. heben	_____	e. to go

E   Schreib einen deutschen Befehl zu jeder Abbildung. *Write a German command for each illustration.*

1. _____

2. _____

3. _____

4. _____

5. _____

F Ergänze jeden Satz. *Complete each sentence.*

1. _____ Papier heraus.

2. Sag das _____ deutsch.

3. _____ dich.

4. Mach das _____ zu.

5. _____ die Hand.

6. Ergänze die _____.

7. _____ das Buch.

G Wähle den zutreffenden Befehl! *Choose the corresponding command.*

1. Write.   (Sprich!   Schreib!   Hör zu!)
2. Raise.   (Heb!   Lies!   Mach zu!)
3. Speak.   (Geh!   Ergänze!   Sprich!)
4. Say.   (Mach auf!   Setz dich! Sag!)
5. Take out. (Nimm heraus! Hör zu!   Geh!)

BITTE NUR IM
WASSER FÜTTERN

NICHT NUR HUNDE
VERUNREINIGEN DIE WEGE

Fahrräder bitte
am Südwall
abstellen
←

PARKSCHEIN-
AUTOMAT
Hier Parkschein
lösen

nie ohne!
Im Verbund-Verkehr vor dem Einsteigen
Fahrschein
am Automaten ziehen. Nachlösen unmöglich.
Schwarzfahrer zahlen 40,-DM.

Fahr
vorsichtig

Es könnte auch
Dein Kind sein

Hier
Rundfahrten!
DAUER: CA. 1 STUNDE
Fahrpreis DM 5,00

NUMBERS
Zahlen

Wieviel ist...?   How much is...?

1 eins
2 zwei
3 drei
4 vier
5 fünf

6 sechs
7 sieben
8 acht
9 neun
10 zehn

11 elf
12 zwölf
13 dreizehn
14 vierzehn
15 fünfzehn

16 sechzehn
17 siebzehn
18 achtzehn
19 neunzehn

20 zwanzig
21 einundzwanzig
22 zweiundzwanzig
23 dreiundzwanzig
24 vierundzwanzig
25 fünfundzwanzig
26 sechsundzwanzig
27 siebenundzwanzig
28 achtundzwanzig
29 neunundzwanzig

30 dreißig
31 einunddreißig
32 zweiunddreißig

40 vierzig
41 einundvierzig
42 zweiundvierzig

50 fünfzig
51 einundfünfzig
52 zweiundfünfzig

60 sechzig
61 einundsechzig
62 zweiundsechzig

70 siebzig
71 einundsiebzig
72 zweiundsiebzig

80 achtzig
81 einundachtzig
82 zweiundachtzig

90 neunzig
91 einundneunzig
92 zweiundneunzig

100 hundert
200 zweihundert
1.000 tausend

Ein Narr kann mehr fragen als sieben Weise sagen.

One fool can ask more questions than seven wise men can answer.

Supplementary Vocabulary

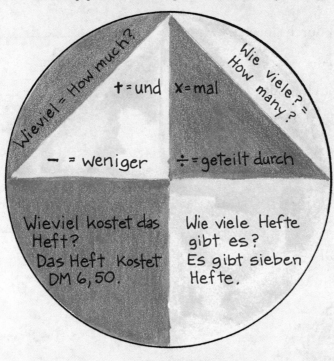

Wieviel = How much?

+ = und

x = mal

Wie viele? = How many?

— = weniger

÷ = geteilt durch

Wieviel kostet das Heft?
Das Heft kostet DM 6,50.

Wie viele Hefte gibt es?
Es gibt sieben Hefte.

Exercises

A After you study the numbers and practice saying them, try to write these numbers from memory. (Auf deutsch, bitte.)

1 _____   6 _____

2 _____   7 _____

3 _____   8 _____

4 _____   9 _____

5 _____   10 _____

B Rate yourself. How did you do? Circle your evaluation.

1. very well   2. fairly well   3. poorly

C Practice again. Schreib die Zahlen! *Write the numbers.*

　　　Beispiel: zwei __2__

1. fünf _____   4. neun _____

2. acht _____   5. sieben _____

3. eins _____

D Schreib das deutsche Wort für jede Zahl!

3 _____   6 _____

4 _____   10 _____

E Tell whether the following equations indicate addition, subtraction, multiplication or division.

1. Vierzehn geteilt durch sieben ist zwei. _____

2. Zwei und zehn ist zwölf. _____

3. Acht mal drei ist vierundzwanzig. _____

4. Neunzehn weniger dreizehn ist sechs. _____

F Try once more to write the numbers in German. (Auf deutsch, bitte.)

8 _____ 3 _____ 10 _____ 1 _____ 9 _____

2 _____ 5 _____ 4 _____ 7 _____ 6 _____

G Wie viele Objekte gibt es hier? *How many objects are pictured? Write the number in German.*

= _____

= _____

= _____

= _____

= _____

H Wie viele Objekte gibt es zusammen? *How many* _____
objects are there altogether?

Now, write this sum in German. _____

I Schreib die Antworten auf deutsch!

     Beispiel: 6 − 4 = <u>zwei</u>

1.   12 × 4 = _____
2.   30 − 10 = _____
3.   8 − 6 = _____
4.   12 + 18 = _____
5.   100 ÷ 2 = _____
6.   60 + 10 = _____
7.   30 − 15 = _____
8.   80 ÷ 2 = _____
9.   10 × 10 = _____
10. 15 + 4 = _____

J Your teacher will say ten numbers in German. Write the corresponding numbers.

1. _____   6. _____
2. _____   7. _____
3. _____   8. _____
4. _____   9. _____
5. _____   10. _____

K How many interior angles are there in each design? Circle the number.

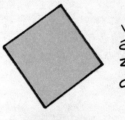

vier
acht
zehn
drei

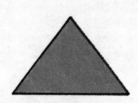

fünf
drei
vier
sieben

sieben
sechs
elf
fünf

fünf
neun
acht
elf

L Lies den Absatz! *Read the paragraph. Dann wähle die richtigen Antworten!*

Im Klassenzimmer gibt es viele Objekte. Es gibt fünfundzwanzig Stühle, vier Fenster, sieben Wischer, neunzehn Hefte und eine Karte. Ein Stuhl kostet siebenundzwanzig Dollar. Ein Wischer kostet fünfunddreißig Cents und eine Karte kostet vierzig Dollar.

1. Im Klassenzimmer gibt es...Objekte.
    a. wenige   c. acht
    b. viele   d. zehn

2. Es gibt insgesamt (totally)...Objekte.
    a. einundvierzig   c. sechsundfünfzig
    b. achtunddreißig   d. dreiundzwanzig

3. Wieviel kostet ein Stuhl?
    a. $27.00   c. $40.00
    b. $35.00   d. $25.00

4. Wie viele Hefte gibt es?
    a. 53   c. 25
    b. 7   d. 19

5. Wie viele Fenster gibt es?
    a. 19   c. 4
    b. 25   d. 9

Kreuzworträtsel

M

Vertical

2. lucky number in dice
3. 10, 8, 6, 4, . . . , 0, −2
4. April, June and September have a total of . . . days.
5. 10 centuries = . . . years
9. sechs . . . zwei = acht
10. He started first grade when he was . . . years old.
12. mathematical word for minus
13. one dozen
15. two numbers after "neun"
17. Reverse this number and it's still the same.
18. square root of nine
20. "Ein . . ." asks many foolish questions.

Horizontal

1. Self multiplied, it is unchanged.
3. 1800 ÷ 9 = . . .
6. how many
7. square of three
8. Its square is twenty-five.
11. After "neunzehn" comes . . . .
14. "geteilt . . ."
16. word for this sign: ×
18. two and one half dozen = . . . (ß = ss)
19. ¼ of 60
21. square of two or square root of sixteen
22. "Wieviel . . . ?"
23. ⅖ of 100

Notruf/Polizei	**1 10**
Feuer/Rettungsdienst	**1 12**
Krankentransporte	**3 50 11**
Soforthilfe bei Brand- und Wasserschaden	**3 37 43**

Deutschland in Zahlen

Die Deutschen in Zahlen – nachzulesen im Statistischen Jahrbuch 1993 (1200 Seiten): ● Die **Bevölkerung** im Westen nahm 1991 um 620 000 Menschen zu (64,07 Mio.), die im Osten dagegen um rund 200 000 ab (15,91 Mio.) ● In den 35,3 Millionen deutschen **Haushalten** leben zu rund 33 % Singles und in 31 % 2 Personen. Nur in 5 % mehr als 5 Menschen. ● 50 % der Haushalte hat ein **Einkommen** von weniger als 2500 Mark, nur 3,4 % mehr als 7500 Mark. ● Die Summe aller **Sozialleistungen** betrug 1992 erstmals mehr als eine Billion (1000 Milliarden) Mark: 87 % für den Westen, nur 12 % für die neuen Länder.

Schulferien in Niedersachsen

Ostern	27. 03. (Sa)	–	17. 04.	(Sa)
Pfingsten	29. 05. (Sa)	–	01. 06.	(Di)
Sommer	18. 06. (Fr)	–	31. 07.	(Sa)
Herbst	24. 09. (Fr)	–	02. 10.	(Sa)
Weihnachten	23. 12. (Do)	–	08. 01	(Sa)

GEOGRAPHY
Geographie

5

Andere Länder,
andere Sitten.

when in Rome, do
as the Romans do.

Deutschland (Germany)

Berlin, the capital of Germany, is a publishing and fashion center and home of the Berlin Philharmonic Orchestra and the Dahlem Museum. Berlin is also the site of the Brandenburg Gate and an important cultural center. It is the home of the Brecht Ensemble Theater and the Pergamon Museum with its collection of Classical Greek artifacts.

Bonn, a small city on the Rhine River, is the birthplace of the composer Ludwig van Beethoven.

Köln ("colonia"), a former Roman colony, is an industrial city known for its Gothic cathedral, perfume, "4711-Kölnisch Wasser," and for its annual carnival parade.

Hamburg is the largest seaport of Germany and a major industrial center. It is the site of Hagenbeck's Zoo and many beautiful parks.

München, the site of the *Oktoberfest,* is a major cultural center with art galleries and orchestras.

Leipzig, an industrial and cultural city on the Weiße Elster and the Pleiße Rivers, is a publishing and fur center. It hosts the biannual trade fair *(Leipziger Messe)* and is the home of the Gewandhaus Orchestra and the Church of St. Thomas with its famous Boys' Choir.

Dresden, called the "Florence of the North" because of its many artworks, is an important manufacturing and industrial center. It is known for its *Dresdner Stollen* (Christmas fruit bread) and for its porcelain.

Schweiz (Switzerland)

Bern is the capital of the nation. It is located on the Aare River.

Genf (Geneva) is an international conference center and second home of many international film stars.

Zürich is a famous world banking center.

Switzerland has picturesque resort areas such as the city of Luzern and ski centers such as Gstaad and St. Moritz.

Österreich (Austria)

Wien (Vienna) is the capital city of the nation and a major industrial and cultural center. It is the home of the Vienna Boys' Choir and the Spanish Riding School with its white Lippizan stallions. It is a center of music with opera houses and orchestras.

Salzburg, the birthplace of the composer Wolfgang Amadeus Mozart, is a city that derives its name from a castle and a salt mine. The filming of the motion picture *Sound of Music* took place here.

> "Nordsee" stands for North Sea, but "Ostsee" is called Baltic Sea, not East Sea.

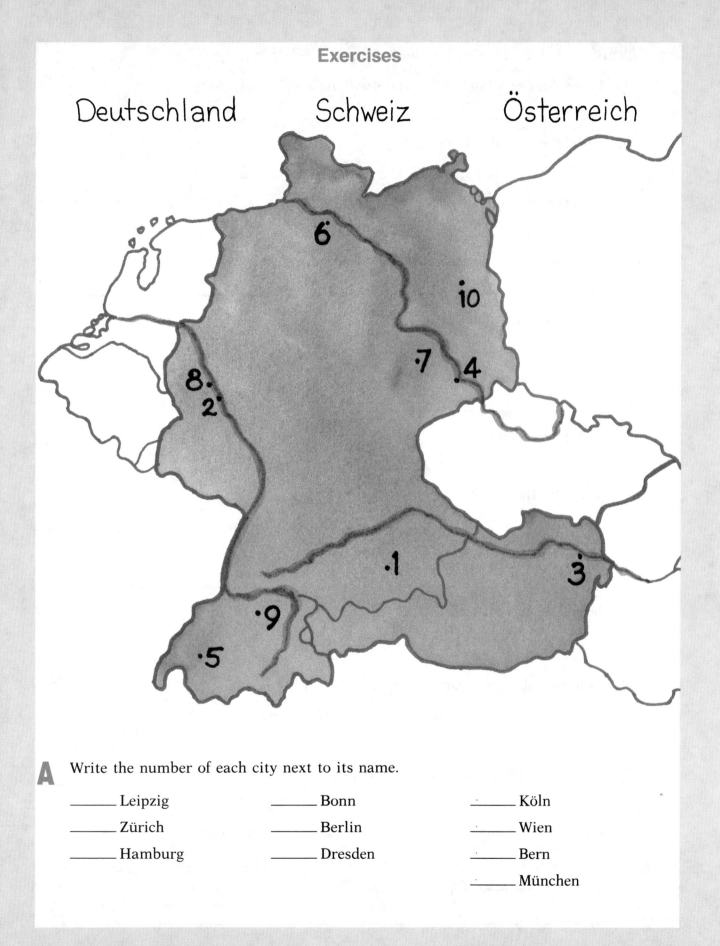

Deutschland   Schweiz   Österreich

A Write the number of each city next to its name.

_____ Leipzig   _____ Bonn   _____ Köln

_____ Zürich   _____ Berlin   _____ Wien

_____ Hamburg   _____ Dresden   _____ Bern

                                                 _____ München

B Identify the cities described in the information below.

1. home of the Spanish Riding School with its white Lippizan stallions

   _____

2. site of the annual "Oktoberfest"

   _____

3. site of the Brandenburg Gate

   _____

4. city noted for perfumes and pleasant fragrances

   _____

5. site of a famous fair twice a year

   _____

6. capital of Switzerland

   _____

7. birthplace of Mozart

   _____

8. site of the Dahlem Museum

   _____

9. city noted for art treasures

   _____

10. largest seaport of Germany

   _____

C After studying the maps carefully, find the following items.

1. one river that forms, in part, the boundary of two countries

   _____

2. one large mountain range which extends over several countries

   _____

3. one river which flows through the cities of Dresden and Hamburg

   _____

4. one lake on the border of two countries

   _____

D Match column B with column A.

	A		**B**
1.	Bonn	_____	a. east of München, close to the German border
2.	Berlin	_____	b. on the southern end of the Elbe
3.	Leipzig	_____	c. on the Donau
4.	Salzburg	_____	d. near the mouth of the Elbe
5.	Wien	_____	e. on the Weiße Elster and Pleiße
6.	Bern	_____	f. north of Dresden and east of the Elbe
7.	Hamburg	_____	g. on the Rhein
8.	Dresden	_____	h. on the Aare

E Nenne die Stadt, die zu jeder Abbildung paßt! *Name the city associated with each picture.*

1. 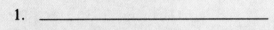 _____

2. _____

3. _____

4. _____

WILLKOMMEN SUMMIT TALKS TODAY

5. _____

F Wähle die richtige Antwort!

1. Wien is the capital of .....
    a. Germany   b. Liechtenstein   c. Switzerland   d. Austria

2. "Harz" is the name of a ....
    a. mountain range   b. city   c. river   d. sea

3. München is a city in the .... of Germany.
    a. south   b. east   c. north   d. west

4. A country that borders Austria to the west is ....
    a. Germany   b. France   c. Switzerland   d. Italy

5. Hamburg is a seaport on the ....
    a. Rhein   b. Donau   c. Aare   d. Elbe

6. Berlin is located .... of Leipzig.
    a. west   b. north   c. east   d. south

7. Poland lies to the .... of Germany.
    a. west   b. north   c. south   d. east

8. Leipzig is a ....
    a. city   b. river   c. country   d. lake

9. The Alps are a ....
    a. country   b. lake   c. mountain range   d. river

10. In Germany, the lowlands are located in the ....
    a. south   b. north   c. east   d. west

G Write in each blank space the answer that makes each statement geographically correct.

Located in northern Europe, Germany has a variety of geographical features. It has two seacoasts, one on the Nordsee or 1._____ and the other on the Ostsee or 2._____. Crossed by canals and dotted with many small lakes, the northern lowlands cover about one-third of the country. Rolling hills and small mountain ranges cover the remaining two-thirds. One centrally located range is the 3._____.

Germany has many neighbors. Far to the north is 4._____ and to the east are 5._____ and 6._____. To the south are two German-speaking nations, 7._____ and 8._____. To the west are 9._____, 10._____, 11._____ and 12._____. Although the nearby principality of 13._____ does not share a border with Germany, it is a close neighbor and shares the language.

In the German-speaking area of Europe there are two capitals which begin with the letter "B." They are 14._____ and 15._____. Two other capitals begin with "V": 16._____ and 17._____ (or "Wien" in German).

The huge mountain range called the 18._____ boasts magnificent scenery, including glaciers and mountain lakes. However, there is always the possibility of avalanches, especially in the spring. Mountain climbing and skiing are popular pastimes in the Alpine countries. Two well-known ski resorts are 19._____ and 20._____.

H Imagine that you must plan an itinerary (list of sightseeing places) for two groups of American tourists. The first group would like to see cultural sites (i.e., things or places pertaining to music, art, or theater). The second group would like to see athletic events and visit recreational resorts. Which places would you suggest for each group and why?

Group 1

_____

_____

_____

_____

_____

_____

_____

Group 2

_____

_____

_____

_____

_____

_____

_____

Maze

Marianne and Michael are ready to travel. Trace their vacation route to find out where they will be spending the summer. Name their destination in the space provided. List the places they will visit while en route.

Places they'll visit:

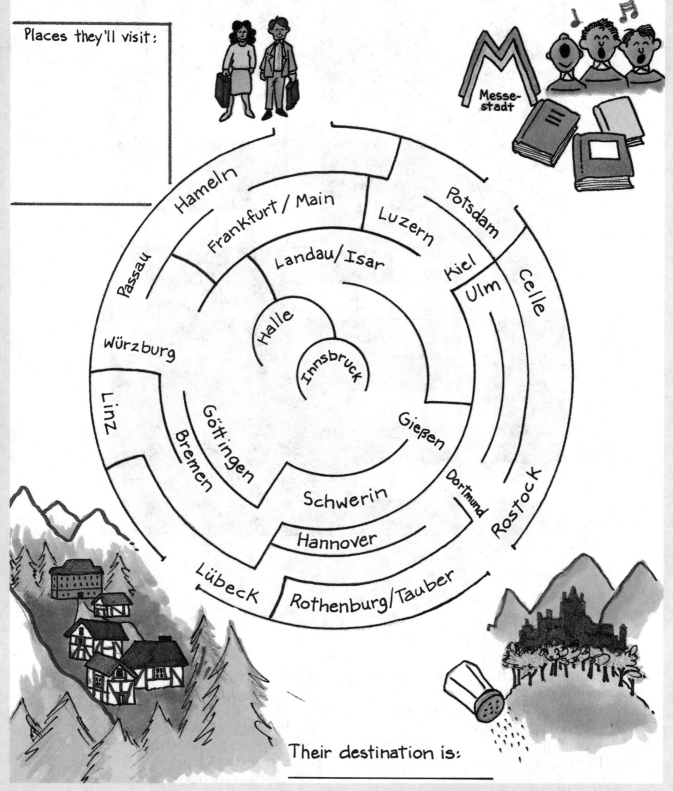

Messe-stadt

Their destination is:

_____

Kreuzworträtsel

J

Vertical

1. capital city on the Danube (German spelling)
3. site of the Gewandhaus Orchestra
5. long navigable river
7. mountain range
8. birthplace of Mozart

Horizontal

2. another long navigable river (German spelling)
4. "Florence of the North"
6. banking center of Switzerland
9. seaport and industrial center
10. city on the Rhine
11. capital city of Germany

Freundliches München
Munich smiles

Rhein
Montabaur
Köln
Koblenzer Kreuz
Güls
Winningen
Koblenz
Bonn
Wiesbaden
Kobern
Lehmen
Kattenes
Alken
Löf
Burg Eltz
Hatzenport
Brodenbach
bfahrt Kaisersesch
Karden
Treis
Klotten
Valwig
Bruttig Fankel
Beilstein
Cochem
Ernst
Ellen Ediger
Briedern
Eller
Mesenich
Senheim
Bremm
Neef
St. Aldegund
Alf
Bullay
Zell/Mosel
Briedel
fahrt Ulmen
Reil
underich skirch
Kröv
Traben-Trarbach
ürzig
Mosel
Eifel
Hunsrück

Hessen		
	Mainz	
Hauptstadt:	19849 km^2	
Fläche:	3,7 Millionen	
Einwohner:		

Rheinland-Pfalz	
Hauptstadt:	
Fläche:	
Einwohner:	Wiesbaden
	21114 km^2
	5,7 Millionen

Saarland	Saarbrücken
	2570 km^2
Hauptstadt:	1,1 Millionen
Fläche:	
Einwohner:	

HAUPTSTADT BERLIN

ORANIENBURG
FALKENSEE
REINICKENDORF
PANKOW
WEISSENSEE
HOHEN-SCHÖN-HAUSEN
WEDDING
SPANDAU
PRENZ-LAUER BERG
MARZAHN
LICHTEN-BERG
HELLERS-DORF
STRAUSSBERG
CHARLOTTEN-BURG
TIER-GAR-TEN
MITTE
FRIED-RICHS-HAIN
WILMERSDORF
KREUZ-BERG
SCHÖNE-BERG
NEU-KÖLLN
TEM-PEL-HOF
ZEHLENDORF
STEGLITZ
KÖPENICK
POTSDAM
TELTOW
MAHLOW

Bis bald in
Eschwege

HOUSE
Haus

6

Monika: Wo wohnst du?
Andreas: Ich wohne in einem Haus in Dresden.

Stefan: Wo ist der Garten?
Gisela: Der Garten ist da drüben.

Bettina: Wo sind die Garagen?
Kurt: Sie sind hinter dem Garten.

Karin: Wie viele Zimmer gibt es in
    deinem Haus?
Dieter: Es gibt neun Zimmer.

Where do you live?
I live in a house in Dresden.

Where is the garden?
The garden is over there.

Where are the garages?
They are behind the garden.

How many rooms are there in
your house?
There are nine rooms.

die Zimmer im Haus

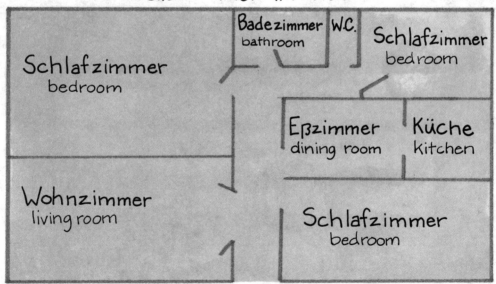

 Wenn die Katze aus dem Haus
ist, tanzen die Mäuse.

When the cat's away,
the mice will play.

Villa

Einfamilienhaus

Mietshaus

Wohnung

Wohnwagen

Hütte

Zelt

A Schreib das deutsche Wort für jedes Zimmer!

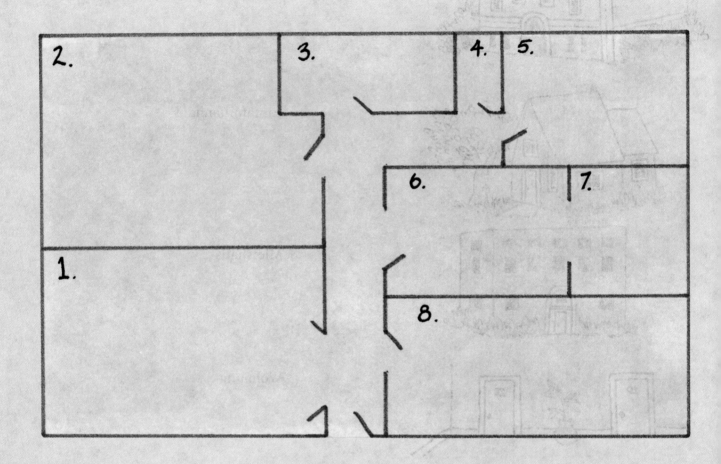

B Ergänze die Sätze!

1. Ich <u>koche</u> in der _____.
   (to cook)

2. Ich <u>schlafe</u> in dem _____.
   (to sleep)

3. Ich <u>esse</u> in dem _____.
   (to eat)

4. Ich <u>bade</u> in dem _____.
   (to bathe)

5. Ich <u>wohne</u> in dem _____.
   (to live)

6. Ich <u>spiele</u> in dem _____.
   (to play)

C Wähle das richtige Zimmer!

1. Wohnzimmer   (bathroom   kitchen   living room)
2. Schlafzimmer (dining room   bedroom   bathroom)
3. Badezimmer   (living room   bathroom   bedroom)
4. Eßzimmer   (dining room   kitchen   living room)
5. Küche   (bedroom   living room   kitchen)

D In which room would you find a . . . (Auf deutsch, bitte.)

1. bed? _____

2. stove? _____

3. sofa? _____

4. toothbrush? _____

5. dining table? _____

E Complete each sentence with the appropriate German word.

1. If you went camping, you would sleep in a

_____.

2. If you lived in an apartment, you would call it a

_____.

3. If you lived in a single house, you would call it an

_____.

4. If you lived in a large beautiful house, you would call it a

_____.

5. If you found a rough shelter in the woods, you would call it a

_____.

6. If you slept in a mobile residence, you would call it a

_____.

F Schreib die Wörter richtig! *Unscramble the words.*

1. ELTZ _____

2. MEIMZR _____

3. ÜKECH _____

4. ASHU _____

5. TRAGEN _____

HAUS   FAMILIE   LIEBE

G Lies den Absatz. Wähle die richtigen Antworten!

Hier ist mein Haus. Es ist schön. Meine Familie wohnt hier. Ich liebe meine Familie und mein Haus. Das Haus hat sieben Zimmer. Hinter dem Haus ist der Garten.

1. Meine Familie wohnt....
   - a. Zimmer
   - b. in einem Haus
   - c. Liebe
   - d. Garten

2. Mein Haus ist....
   - a. neu
   - b. alt
   - c. schön
   - d. klein

3. Mein Haus hat...Zimmer.
   - a. fünf
   - b. sechs
   - c. sieben
   - d. acht

4. Der Garten ist hinter dem....
   - a. Haus
   - b. Familie
   - c. Zimmer
   - d. Garten

H

Vertical

1. place to bathe
2. place to live
3. located in a "Mietshaus"
4. simple wooden building
6. found in all residences
7. large luxurious house

Horizontal

3. house on wheels
5. place to prepare meals
6. canvas shelter
8. "...haus," kind of house
9. place to play or to plant flowers

zum Beispiel
Wohn-
zimmer
JUBILÄUMS-
PREISE!

zum Beispiel
Speise-
zimmer
JUBILÄUMS-
PREISE!

BIEN-HAUS Harmonie
Gründau

Erfahrung und Können. Überzeugend
überträgt sich der äußere Eindruck auf die
inneren Werte. Überraschende Perspektiven,
großzügige Präsenz.

zum Beispiel
Schlaf-
zimmer
JUBILÄUMS-
PREISE!

zum Beispiel
Jugend-
zimmer
JUBILÄUMS-
PREISE!

ALLE KUCKY-KÜCHEN SIND VOLL ERWEITERUNGSFÄHIG

Der Kucky-Küchen-Hit in hellbeigem Kunststoff mit Buche Nachbildung an den Bügelgriffen, weißer Elektroherd mit Edelstahl Kochmulde, Dunstabzugshaube und Spülbecken!

2498,-
KUCKY-ABHOLPREIS
inkl. aller Elektrogeräte
Finanzkaufpreis: 9 x 263,- · 1 x 271,- = 2.638,-

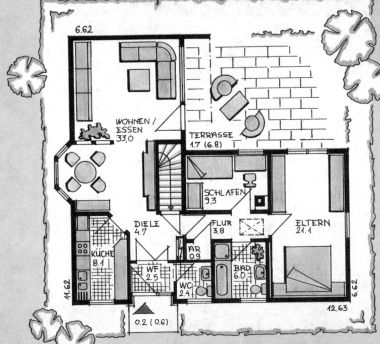

Vermietungen

1- u. 2-Zimmer-Appartements
Hannoversche Str. 152 – Erstbezug –
Kochn., DU/WC, Blk./Terr., ab DM 350,- zzgl. Nebenkosten
ab 1. Oktober 1993 zu vermieten.
Bes.: Mo.–Fr. 11.00–14.00 u. Sa. 10.00–11.00 Uhr

Wohnungsmarkt, Telefon: 5 40 55

1- u. 2-Zi.-Wohnungen
Valentinsbreite 17–23/
Nähe Klinikum
ab sof. zu verm., ab DM 450,-
zzgl. NK/HZ.
Wohnungsmarkt, Tel. 5 40 55

Wohnen auf Zeit
MitWohnZentrale – Kuhlmeier & Schulze Gbr
Tel. 05 51/19 44 45, ∅ Fax 4 71 58
3-7W Kü., Bad, Gartenben., 70 m², renov. Altbau 785,- + NK
Gashzg., Nähe Stettiner Str.
Lutze Wohnungsvermittlung, Bühlstr. 5, Tel. 4 62 22

Studentenverbindung vermietet
Zimmer an interessierte Studenten.
☎ 5 95 91

1-Zimmer-Whg.
Ko., Bad, Blk.
Bovenden, Steffensweg 94
ab sofort zu verm.
ab DM 390,- + NK/HZ.
Wohnungsmarkt, Tel. 5 40 55

Immobilienmarkt
Zu verk.: 1-Zi.-Whg. 34,09 m²,
Stadtmitte Gö., VP 135 000,-.
☎ (0 71 51) 2 34 90

FAMILY
Familie

Markus: Wer ist das?	Who is that?
Heidi: Das ist mein <u>Bruder</u>.	That's my <u>brother</u>.
Rudi: Wer sind die Kinder?	Who are the children?
Stefan: Sie sind meine <u>Enkelkinder.</u>	They are my <u>grandchildren</u>.
Sabine: Sind das deine <u>Eltern</u>?	Are they your <u>parents</u>?
Evelyn: Ja, meine <u>Mutter</u> heißt Judith und mein <u>Vater</u> heißt Josef.	Yes, my <u>mother's</u> name is Judith and my <u>father's</u> name is Josef.
Christl: Renate und Brigitte sind <u>Schwestern</u> nicht wahr?	Renate and Brigitte are <u>sisters</u>, aren't they?
Werner: Ja, und sie sind auch meine <u>Kusinen</u>.	Yes, and they are also my <u>cousins</u>.

Vergiß nicht: Familientreffen-Gäste: • Großvater, Großmutter • Tante Rosalinda und ihr Mann • Kusine Marille • Cousin Lorenz • meine Schwester und ihre Kinder • Andreas und seine Frau • Gisela und das Baby	Don't forget: Family Reunion-Guests: • grandfather, grandmother • Aunt Rosalinda and her husband • Cousin Marille • Cousin Lorenz • my sister and her children • Andreas and his wife • Gisela and the baby

Hanni: Wo sind deine Verwandten?	Where are your relatives?
Franz: Meine <u>Großeltern</u> sind drinnen und meine <u>Tanten</u> und <u>Onkel</u> sind im Garten.	My <u>grandparents</u> are inside and my <u>aunts</u> and <u>uncles</u> are in the garden.
Lynnie: Sind deine <u>Paten</u> hier?	Are your <u>godparents</u> here?
Susanna: Ja, sicher. Meine <u>Patin</u> spricht gerade mit meinen Tanten. Mein Pate ist auf der Terrasse.	Yes, of course. My <u>godmother</u> is speaking with my aunts. My <u>godfather</u> is on the terrace.
Eberhard: Wie heißen dein <u>Neffe</u> und deine <u>Nichte</u>?	What are the names of your <u>nephew</u> and your <u>niece</u>?
Hans: Mein Neffe heißt Axel und meine Nichte heißt Michaela.	My nephew's name is Arel and my niece's name is Michaela.
Lars: Bist du ihr einziger <u>Onkel</u>?	Are you their only uncle?
Peter: Nein, auch Michael ist ihr Onkel.	No, Michael is also their uncle.

Kinder und Narren sprechen die Wahrheit.	Children and fools speak the truth.

das Mädchen — girl
das Kind — child
der Junge — boy
die Tochter — daughter
der Sohn — son
die Enkelin — granddaughter
der Enkel — grandson

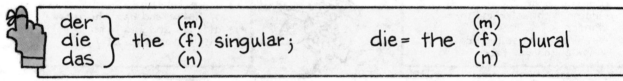

der
die } the (m) (f) (n) singular;   die = the (m) (f) (n) plural
das

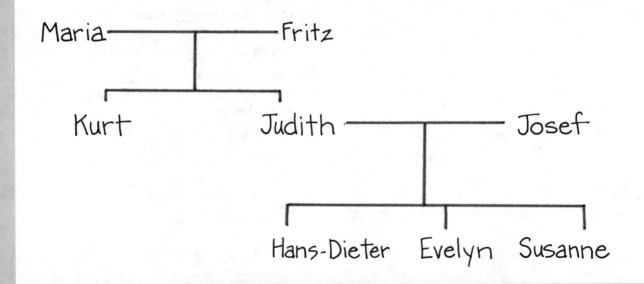

Maria —————————— Fritz

Kurt   Judith ————————— Josef

Hans-Dieter   Evelyn   Susanne

Exercises

A Indicate Susanne's relationship to each family member listed.

Susanne ist die

1. _____Schwester_____ von Evelyn.
2. _____ von Hans-Dieter.
3. _____ von Josef.
4. _____ von Maria.
5. _____ von Kurt.
6. _____ von Fritz.
7. _____ von Judith.

B Tu nun das Gleiche für Judith und Fritz! *Now do the same for Judith and Fritz.*

Judith ist die

1. _____ von Susanne, Hans-Dieter und Evelyn.
2. _____ von Josef.
3. _____ von Kurt.
4. _____ von Fritz und Maria.

Fritz ist der

1. _____ von Maria.
2. _____ von Judith und Kurt.
3. _____ von Hans-Dieter, Evelyn und Susanne.

C Wer ist das? *Who is that?* (Auf deutsch, bitte.)

1. "Bruder" of my "Vater" _____

2. "Sohn" of my "Tante" _____

3. "Mutter" of my "Mutter" _____

4. "Tochter" of my "Onkel" _____

5. "Sohn" of my "Eltern" _____

D Wer bin ich? *Who am I?* (Auf deutsch, bitte.)

1. I am your cousin's mother.
   In other words, I am your _____.
2. I am your father's brother.
   In other words, I am your _____.
3. I am your male sibling.
   In other words, I am your _____.
4. I am your offspring.
   In other words, I am your _____.

E Wähle die richtige Antwort!

1. Wo ist das Kind?
   a. on the bench
   b. in the playpen
   c. in the foreground

2. Wo sind die Großeltern?
   a. on the bench
   b. in the playpen
   c. in the foreground

3. Wo sind die Eltern?
   a. on the bench
   b. in the playpen
   c. in the foreground

F   Schreib auf englisch!

1. Wer ist das? _____

2. Wer singt? _____

3. Wer ist der Mann? _____

4. Wer kommt zu der Party? _____

G   Ergänze auf deutsch!

1. Wer ist der Junge? (son)
   Der Junge ist mein _____.
2. Wer ist die Frau? (mother)
   Die Frau ist meine _____.
3. Wer ist das Mädchen? (niece)
   Das Mädchen ist meine _____.

H   Lies den Absatz. Schreib den Absatz auf englisch! *Read the paragraph. Write it in English.*

Meine Familie

Ich habe eine kleine Familie. Mein Vater ist sechsunddreißig Jahre alt. Meine Mutter ist siebenunddreißig Jahre alt. Meine Schwester heißt Ingrid und sie ist acht. Mein Bruder heißt Hans und er ist fünf. Ich heiße Patricia. Meine Familie wohnt in Lübeck und meine Großeltern wohnen in Berlin.

> wohnen – to live, reside

_____

_____

_____

_____

_____

_____

13. MAI MUTTERTAG

In Liebe und Dankbarkeit nehmen wir Abschied
von unserer lieben Mutter, Oma und Uroma

Hilda Bortmann

geb. 21. Sept. 1913   gest. 4. Okt. 1993

In stiller Trauer:
Sohn Manfred und Ehefrau Hannelore
Tochter Inge und Ehemann Jupp
Sohn Lutz und Ehefrau Ursula
ihre Enkelkinder und Urenkel
sowie alle, die ihr im Leben nahestanden
Die Trauerfeier findet am 11. 10. 1993, 14.00 Uhr
auf dem Friedhof Gohlis statt.

Ein Baby ist angekommen!

Herzliche Glückwünsche

Dem Brautpaar zur Vermählung herzliche Glückwünsche

In Gemünden Herrn Franz Matuschka, St.-Bruno-Straße 14, zum 85. Geburtstag.
In Adelsberg Herrn Johann Meltsch, Diemarstraße 12, zum 75. Geburtstag.

8 OCCUPATIONS
Berufe

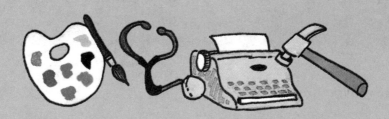

Was ist dein Beruf ?
Ich bin Schauspieler.
Was machst du ?
Ich bin Schauspielerin.

What is your occupation?
I am an actor.
What do you do? (for a living)
I am an actress.

der Arzt	m }	physician
die Ärztin	f }	
der Koch	m }	cook
die Köchin	f }	
der Geschäftsmann	m }	businessman
die Geschäftsfrau	f }	businesswoman

Acme Arbeitsvermittlung
sucht :

Tischler, -in   Künstler, -in
Musiker, -in   Lehrer, -in
Mechaniker, -in   Elektriker, -in
Landwirt, -in   Briefträger, -in
Klempner, -in   Krankenpfleger, -in

Arbeitsstellen garantiert.
Tel. 12-59-43

Acme Employment Agency
is looking for:

carpenter   artist
musician   teacher
mechanic   electrician
farmer   letter carrier
plumber   nurse

Work guaranteed.
Tel. 12-59-43

 Jeder ist seines
Glückes Schmied.

One forges one's own
destiny.

Exercises

A Number in order the professions or trades as your teacher recites them.

die Ärztin _____   der Lehrer _____

der Geschäftsmann _____   die Mechanikerin _____

die Künstlerin _____   der Koch _____

der Landwirt _____   der Klempner _____

die Briefträgerin _____   die Musikerin _____

B Wer arbeitet hier? *Who works here?*

1. stage _____

2. dairy farm _____

3. post office _____

4. recording studio _____

5. studio _____

6. hospital _____

7. kitchen _____

8. wood shop _____

9. school _____

10. garage _____

C Schreib die Wörter richtig.

1. RELRHE _____

2. TIRDWALN _____

3. ITZÄRN _____

4. INCHÖK _____

5. PLNERKEM _____

52

D Wie heißt das auf englisch? *Write the sentences in English. Look first, then take a good guess.*

1. Mein Vater ist Mechaniker.

   _____

2. Er repariert Autos.

   _____

3. Meine Mutter ist Sekretärin.

   _____

4. Sie tippt Briefe.

   _____

5. Mein Onkel ist Lehrer.

   _____

6. Er lehrt.

   _____

7. Meine Tante ist Briefträgerin.

   _____

8. Sie bringt Briefe.

   _____

E Guess who. . .(Auf deutsch, bitte.)

1. Der _____ instructs students

2. Die _____ is in charge of the (medical) operation.

3. Der _____ checks for faulty wiring.

4. Die _____ installs water pipes.

5. Der _____ paints portraits.

6. Die _____ cooks food.

7. Der _____ manages a company.

8. Die _____ milks cows.

9. Der _____ delivers mail.

10. Die _____ plays in a symphony orchestra.

F Schreib einen Beruf zu jeder Abbildung!

1. _____

2. _____

3. _____

4. _____

5. _____

FV AKTUELL
Fachvermittlung
für besonders
qualifizierte Fach-
und Führungskräfte

3017
Diplom-Ingenieur Maschinenbau

48, mobil; langj. In- und Auslandserfahrung im Bereich Flug-
zeug- und Fahrzeugbau; Muttersprache Englisch, Französisch
und Deutsch sehr gut;

sucht neuen verantwortungsvollen Wirkungskreis im Bereich
Vertrieb.

Auskünfte gibt: Herr Muschenich
Fachvermittlungsdienst München,
Kapuzinerstraße 26, 8000 München 2,
☎ 0 89/51 54 - 21 49, Telefax 0 89/51 54 - 66 66

3018
Journalist, PR-Manager

Ende 40, erfahren, routiniert in der Pressearbeit, erworben in
Dienstleistung, Industrie und Presseagentur; Kenntnisse in DTP,
Text- und Bildbearbeitung (Macintosh), Fotografie und
Dokumentation;

sucht verantwortungsvollen Aufgabenbereich,. möglichst
München oder Bayern.

Auskünfte gibt: Herr Kimmeringer
Fachvermittlungsdienst München,
Kapuzinerstraße 26, 8000 München 2,
☎ 0 89/51 54 - 21 97, Telefax 0 89/51 54 - 66 66

3019
Fachübersetzer Englisch, Sprachendienstleiter

25, Berufserfahrung, Erstellung techn. Wörterbücher, Werbe-
schriften, Bedienungsanleitungen, Normen usw. für Kraft-
werks-, Energie- und Verfahrenstechnik sowie Umweltschutz;

sucht Stelle mit hohem Anforderungsprofil, möglichst Süd-
deutschland.

Auskünfte gibt: Herr Kimmeringer
Fachvermittlungsdienst München,
Kapuzinerstraße 26, 8000 München 2,
☎ 0 89/51 54 - 21 97, Telefax 0 89/51 54 - 66 66

3020
Softwareentwickler, Org.-Programmierer

42, verh., Diplom-Physiker Univ. Klausenburg 1972; Weiter-
bildung in EDV; berufliche Kenntn.: COBOL, FORTRAN,
PASCAL, Graphentheorie, Datenstrukturen, SW-Engineering,
PC-Kenntnisse, MS-DOS, Petrinetze; Erfahrung im Unterricht
(Informatik), Rechenzentrum, Projekte in der Wirtschaft;

sucht ausbaufähige Tätigkeit in der Industrie oder Wirtschaft.

Auskünfte gibt: Herr Eisenmann
Fachvermittlungsdienst Nürnberg, Richard-Wagner-Patz 5,
8500 Nürnberg, ☎ 09 11/2 42 -21 41, Telefax 09 11/2 42 -29 99

3021
Diplom-Ingenieur (FH) Elektrotechnik

28, led., mobil, Energieanlagenelektroniker; Diplom FH Osnabrück 8/92, Fachrichtung: Meß-, Steuer- und Regeltechnik
sowie Prozeßautomatisierung; Erfahrung im Softwareentwurf
mit C, ASSEMBLER, PASCAL und in der Mikrocontroller-
Programmierung; Kenntnisse im Platinenentwurf (Eagle);
Englisch gut, Italienisch Grundkenntnisse.

Wunsch: Tätigkeit in Fertigung o. Entwicklung, Produktion
oder Inbetriebnahme/Montage.

Auskünfte gibt: Frau Forstner
Fachvermittlungsdienst Osnabrück, Hamburger Straße 7,
4500 Osnabrück, ☎ 05 41/9 80 - l 64, Telefax 05 41/9 80 - 3 24

TOP-JOB

Fleißige Mitarbeiter gesucht,
die täglich 200,- DM und
mehr verdienen wollen.

Tel. 54 70 13 32 (8–12 Uhr)

Handwerk

BH   Bauhandwerk

astraplan
Fachunternehmen
für Putz & Estrich
Wir sind Ihre
Partner für:
Innenputz & Außenputz, Fassadengestaltung
& Vollwärmeschutz, Estriche & Innenausbau
– lassen Sie sich unverbindlich informieren!
Tel. (030) 784 86 52

Decken, Wände, Fußböden, Dachausbau.
Westerhoff KG, 822 28 38/821 42 46
Fassaden-Verkleidung wärmedämmend,
wartungsfrei, Edelputz/Klinkerstruktu-
ren. Westerhoff KG, 822 28 38/821 42 46

FL   Fliesenarbeiten

Firma Kohndrow, Badmodernisierung
von A-Z, Tel. 801 22 97

FU   Fußbodenarbeiten

Parkett abziehen, versiegeln, Fachbe-
trieb Bley & Co., 892 86 87

GL   Glaserarbeiten

Glaserei Franke, 625 50 10
Die fahrende Glaserei, 49 0 90

HE   Heizungs- / Lüftungsanlagen

Gunther Zink, Sanitär-Heizung, Bada-
nierung-Reparaturen, Gasgerätewar-
tung, Lohmeyerstr, 20, 10587 Berlin,
Tel.: 341 40 51/52, Fax: 341 04 52
Gas- und Ölheizungsanlagen mit
Elektroarbeiten. Neubau - Austausch -
Wartung. Sauber und schnell? Selbst-
verständlich! Stöckl & Fritz GbR,
030/451 74 56

**MA   Malerarbeiten
Tapezierarbeiten**

Maler- und Tapezierarbeiten führt Klein-
betrieb kurzfristig und fachgerecht aus.
Leerwohnung preiswerter, Kloebbe +
Partner, 611 21 81
Malerarbeiten jeder Größenordnung
führt aus: G. Henning KG, Malermeister,
606 20 41
Maler- und Tapezierarbeiten führt Mei-
sterbetrieb allbezirklich aus: 795 40 48

RA   Radio- und Fernsehtechnik

Die Nr.1 in Berlin **88088**
Fernsehkummer? Jägernummer!
– Berlins größter Fernsehdienst –

Fernsehklagen, Höppner fragen, Mei-
sterbetrieb, Hausreparaturen,
792 59 96/ 791 16 87

DEM LEBEN ZULIEBE
Ihre Spende
auf das Konto
909090
bei allen Banken,
der Sparkasse Bonn und dem
Postscheckamt Köln.
**DEUTSCHE
KREBSHILFE E.V.
BONN**

Maler/Tapezierer

Malermeister
renoviert privat/gewerblich, Büro u. Praxis, Zimmer 4x5 m, Decke streichen, Wände tapezieren,
ab 300,- DM; 5 x 5 ab 350,- DM.
Für Leerwohnungen Sonderpreise.
☎ **402 54 54 / 494 20 33**

Maler nimmt für Wochenenden Aufträge
entgegen. Tel. 01715234956
Billig? Nein, preisgünstig! Malermeister-
betrieb bietet hochwert. Maler, Tapezier-
sowie Fliesen u. Trockenbauarbeiten an,
priv. u. gewerbl. ☎3756867, 0172/6188360,
3358761

Polster- und Dekorationsarbeiten

Polsterhandwerk Fenger-Meisterbetrieb -
Aufarbeitung/Neubezug! ☎4481388
Türpolsterung! Fenster- u. Türenabdich-
tung. Förster, Tel./Fax 4296577

Waschmaschinenreparatur

Waschmaschinen, Kühlschränke neu und
gebraucht mit Garantie, Reparatur-
schnelldienst, 6212097

Wir suchen
TELEFONISTIN

für unsere Zentrale, welche
auch im Empfang tätig ist, den
Postausgang betreut, kleinere
Schreibarbeiten übernimmt,
unser Faxgerät bedient und
gerne im Team arbeitet.

ATP
A C H A M M E R
T R I T T H A R T
P A R T N E R
ARCHITEKTEN UND INGENIEURE

Unser Büro befindet sich am
Prinzregentenplatz (U4) und
wir haben gleitende Arbeits-
zeit.

Gerne erwarten wir Ihre
Bewerbung.

Neherstraße 1
8000 München 80
Tel. 4 55 62-0

Innsbruck, Wien, Salzburg,
München, Leipzig

Arbeitslosigkeit muß nicht sein!

Zur Betreuung unserer Kunden
bieten wir noch

4 Damen und Herren
im Alter von 25 bis 52 Jahren

einen hauptberuflichen, krisenfesten
Arbeitsplatz bei hohen Garantie-
Festbezügen.

**Telefon Leipzig 47 53 71
oder 4 01 11 56
Frau Birgit Helms**

Stadt Nürnberg

Wir suchen
Schulleiterin/Schulleiter

für die Berufliche Schule – Direktorat 2 –.
An der Schule werden gegenwärtig ca. 2600 Auszubildende in den
Ausbildungsberufen der Metalltechnik (Maschinenbau, Werkzeugbau)
und Kraftfahrzeugtechnik unterrichtet.
Erforderlich sind die Lehrbefähigung für das Lehramt an beruflichen
Schulen und eine mehrjährige Tätigkeit im beruflichen Schulwesen.
Gesucht wird eine Persönlichkeit mit ausgeprägten pädagogischen
Fähigkeiten, Führungseigenschaften, Organisationstalent sowie der
Bereitschaft zu konzeptionellem Arbeiten und zur Teamarbeit.
Die Beschäftigung erfolgt im Beamten- bzw. im Angestelltenverhältnis
(Stellenwert: BGr. A 16 bzw. VGr. I BAT).
Bitte senden Sie Ihre Bewerbung mit den üblichen Unterlagen inner-
halb von 3 Wochen an

**Stadt Nürnberg, Personalamt
Postfach, 8500 Nürnberg 1**
Benötigen Sie vorab noch weitere Informationen, erreichen Sie uns
unter Telefon **(09 11) 2 31-25 18.**
Übrigens: Die Stadt Nürnberg fördert die berufliche Gleichstellung der
Frauen und begrüßt es, wenn Frauen sich bewerben.

BAD
Berufsgenossenschaftlicher
Arbeitsmedizinischer Dienst

Der BAD — Maßstab für Leistung in der Arbeitsmedizin
Für unser Zentrum **Erlangen** suchen wir zum 1. 1. 1992 eine

ARZTHELFERIN

als Mutterschaftsvertretung für 1½ Jahre, 20 Stunden wöchentlich, die neben
Erfahrung im Untersuchungsbetrieb, Labor, Herz-/Lungenfunktionsprüfung
auch über Kenntnisse im Verwaltungsbereich verfügt. Führerschein Klasse 3
ist erforderlich.

Die Vergütung sowie die zusätzlichen sozialen Leistungen richten sich nach
einem für den öffentlichen Dienst geltenden Tarifvertrag.

Bitte richten Sie Ihre Bewerbung mit den üblichen Unterlagen an:

**Berufsgenossenschaftlicher Arbeitsmedizinischer Dienst e. V.
Zentrum Erlangen
Rathsberger Straße 4, 8520 Erlangen**

FOOD
Essen

Was gibt's zu essen?	What is there to eat?
Es gibt Salat und Suppe.	There is salad and soup.
Hast du Hunger?	Are you hungry?
Ja. Ich habe Hunger.	Yes. I'm hungry.
Hast du Durst?	Are you thirsty?
Nein. Ich habe keinen Durst.	No. I'm not thirsty.

Patricks Lebensmittel
Getränke — Verkauf

Patrick's Grocery
Beverage — Sale

Patricks Lebensmittel		Patrick's Grocery	
Kaffee „Karib" (½ Kg) DM	5,—	"Caribe" coffee (½ Kg) DM	5.00
Tee (¼ Kg)	3,—	tea (¼ Kg)	3.00
Milch (1 Liter)	2,—	milk (1 liter)	2.00
Schokoladenpulver	1,50	chocolate powder mix	1.50
Mineralwasser (2 Liter)	1,—	mineral water (2 liters)	1.00
Fruchtsaft (Dose)	1,50	fruit juice (can)	1.50

Hannis Ecke
Ländliche Küche

Tagesgericht —— Freitag

Hanni's Corner
Regional Food

Menu of the day —— Friday

Menü	Menu
• Klare Hühnersuppe	• chicken broth
• Kalbsbraten	• roast veal
• grüne Bohnen	• green beans
• Röstkartoffeln	• fried potatoes
• gemischter Salat	• mixed salad
• Nachtisch SF 16,—	• dessert SF 16.—
Bei uns schmeckt's immer!	Always tasty here!

Viele Köche verderben den Brei.	Too many cooks spoil the stew.

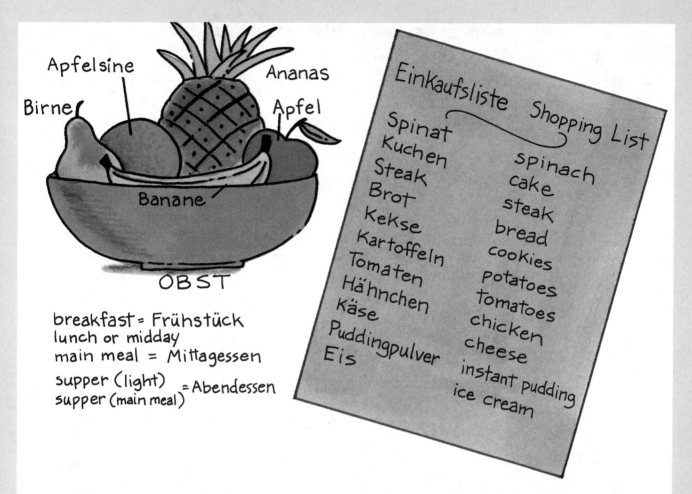

Apfelsine
Birne
Ananas
Apfel
Banane
OBST

Einkaufsliste   Shopping List

Spinat	spinach
Kuchen	cake
Steak	steak
Brot	bread
Kekse	cookies
Kartoffeln	potatoes
Tomaten	tomatoes
Hähnchen	chicken
Käse	cheese
Puddingpulver	instant pudding
Eis	ice cream

breakfast = Frühstück
lunch or midday
main meal = Mittagessen
supper (light)
supper (main meal) = Abendessen

Guten Appetit! — A wish on the part of a friend or host that all the guests may enjoy the meal and eat heartily.

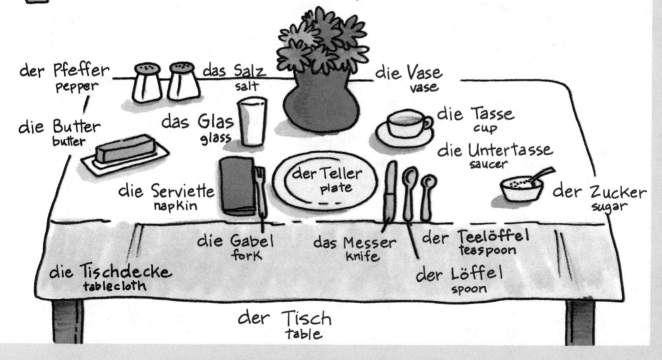

der Pfeffer — pepper
das Salz — salt
die Vase — vase
die Butter — butter
das Glas — glass
die Tasse — cup
die Untertasse — saucer
die Serviette — napkin
der Teller — plate
der Zucker — sugar
die Gabel — fork
das Messer — knife
der Teelöffel — teaspoon
die Tischdecke — tablecloth
der Löffel — spoon
der Tisch — table

Specialties of Germany, Austria and Switzerland

Wiener Schnitzel – breaded and fried veal cutlets; specialty of Vienna, Austria

Sauerbraten – pot roast of marinated beef served with a sour cream gravy and accompanied by red cabbage and potato pancakes

Königsberger Klopse – meatballs flavored with a sauce of cloves, peppercorns, capers and lemon juice and served with buttered noodles; specialty of Königsberg in the former coastal territory of East Prussia

Kartoffelpuffer – potato pancakes prepared with eggs, onion and parsley and fried until golden brown and crispy, served as a main or side dish

Spätzle – noodles made of a flour and egg mixture dropped by the spoon into boiling water and served with butter; specialty of southwestern Germany

Klöße or *Knödel* – dumplings of many varieties used in soups, as side dishes or even as desserts

Lebkuchen – cakes of honey and spices often shaped into hearts and decorated with sayings and proverbs; specialty of Nuremberg (Nürnberg)

Schwarzwälder Kirschtorte – Black Forest Cherry Cake – layer cake with whipped cream, cherry flavored liqueur, cherries and chocolate; specialty of southwestern Germany

Raclette – melted cheese served with boiled potatoes; simple specialty of Switzerland

A Schreib das deutsche Wort für jedes Objekt!

1. _____

2. _____

3. _____

4. _____

5. _____

6. _____

B Ergänze jeden Satz!

1. Potato pancakes are often served with _____.

2. To make "Raclette" one needs to melt _____.

3. "Wiener Schnitzel" is a specialty of _____.

4. A dessert made with honey is _____.

5. The meat of "Sauerbraten" is _____

C Using your food vocabulary list, write three food items for each of the following categories.

meat

1. _____

2. _____

3. _____

vegetables

1. _____

2. _____

3. _____

dairy products

1. _____

2. _____

3. _____

beverages

1. _____

2. _____

3. _____

fruits

1. _____

2. _____

3. _____

desserts

1. _____

2. _____

3. _____

D Answer either 1 or 2 *and* 3 or 4.

1. You are opening a restaurant in Germany. From your food list prepare a menu for lunch and dinner. At least three dishes for each meal should be offered. Specialty dishes may be used.

2. Prepare a poster from magazine pictures. Show a balanced breakfast and a balanced dinner. Label each food with its German name.

3. Prepare 15 different flashcards with a picture of a food item on one side and its German name on the other.

4. List in German 15 words which name a food. Then scramble each word. These can be used in classroom games.
   Example: BIRNE = RIBEN
              EIS = SIE

Kreuzworträtsel

E

Vertical

1. marinated pot roast
2. adds zest to many foods
3. Nuremberg honey cakes
4. other name for "Klöße"
5. One drinks from this.
6. general name for sausage
8. apples, pears, plums
9. Dishes are selected from this.
10. cake
12. served before the main dish
14. orange, tomato, grapefruit
15. often served with milk or tea

Horizontal

1. drop noodles
6. Viennese veal cutlet
7. made from dough for sandwiches
11. name for dumplings (ß = ss)
13. famous Hawaiian fruit
16. evening meal
17. quenched by "Wasser"
18. tossed, fruit, chef's

Gulasch
vom Rind und
Schwein gemischt
1 kg
8.99

3.99

TAGES-MENÜ

gültig von 11.30 – 19 Uhr

vom 13.9. bis 19.9.
vom 11.10. bis 17.10.
vom 8.11. bis 14.11.
vom 6.12. bis 12.12.

Montag *Kartoffelsuppe*
Schnitzel »Wiener Art«
mit frischem Stangenspargel, Sauce Hollandaise
und Petersilienkartoffeln
Rote Grütze mit Sahne
9.80 DM

Dienstag *Broccolicremesuppe*
Holzfällersteak
mit Gewürzgurke und Bratkartoffeln
Schokoladeneis mit Sahne
9.80 DM

Mittwoch *Tomatencremesuppe*
Geschnetzeltes »Züricher Art«
mit Butterspätzle und gemischtem Salat
Zitonencreme
9.80 DM

Donnerstag *Gemüserahmsuppe*
3 Filetmedaillons »Bombay«
mit Sahnecurrysauce, tropischen Früchten
und Butterreis
*Mandelgrießpudding mit
heißen Kirschen*
9.80 DM

Freitag *Rinderkraftbrühe »Frühlingsart«*
Filetmedaillons
mit Rosenkohl, grübnen Bohnen mit Speck
und Kartoffelpürree
Milchreis mit Zimt und Früchten
9.80 DM

Samstag *Spargelcremesuppe*
Schnitzel »à la Nizza«
mit Käse überbacken, Broccoli,
Sauce Bernaise und Croquetten
Apfelmus mit Sahne Häubchen
9.80 DM

Sonntag *Broccolicremesuppe*
Hirschkeulenbraten
in Burgundersauce, Pilzen, Rosenkohl oder
Grünkohl und Petersilienkartoffeln
Vanilleeis mit Sahne
9.80 DM

0.99
Kidney-Bohnen

1.99
Pfirsiche

1.49
Tomaten

**Zimbo
Sandwich
Salami natur**
Ia Spitzenqualität,
100 g

2.49

Bifi
Die Mini-Salami
5 x 25 g-
Packung

3.99

**Bresso
Deutscher
Weichkäse**
sahnig und mild,
60 % Fett i.Tr.,
100 g
1.99

**Holländischer
Gouda jung**
mild und sahnig,
48 % Fett i.Tr.,
100 g
-.79

**St. Mang
Kleinlimburger**
20/40 % Fett i.Tr.,
je 200 g-Stück
2.59

62

ART
Kunst

Three Great Artists
Drei berühmte Künstler

Albrecht Dürer (1471–1528) used his study of Classical art to draw the human form realistically. This Renaissance artist from Nürnberg also used his skills to portray nature exactly. Dürer was equally masterful at wood carving, copper engraving and drawing. His style is Classical, with much attention paid to actual proportion. Like those of other artists of his time, his works frequently used religious themes or reflected his concern about war. *The Young Hare, Saint Anthony* and *The Four Horsemen* are three of his famous works.

Caspar David Friedrich (1774-1840), a North German painter from Greifswald, is an important artist of the Romantic School. He found little need to learn from the Classical masters of Rome, but gathered his inspiration from nature and the beauty of his native countryside. Friedrich was captivated by the contrariness of nature. He realized that nature could be at one time peaceful and at another time violent. He also knew that nature had a charming side and a cruel side. Landscapes and seascapes offered this great artist the means to express this viewpoint. In *Ships in the Harbor of Greifswald*, the viewer might say, the sunrise promises to drive away the gloom and the mystery of night. Or, the viewer might say, the shadows of evening threaten the peacefulness of the ships at anchor. In the *Lone Tree*, the serenity of the vast landscape is disturbed by the sight of a once majestic old tree which has been devastated by lightning.

Ernst Ludwig Kirchner (1880–1938) studied art at the Dresden Technical School. He experimented with both oils and woodcuts and was successful at both. He was convinced that art was being strangled by Romanticism and modern society. To remedy this, he founded a community of artists called the "Bridge" or "Brücke". His group tried to express the frantic pace of modern city life. A good example of this Expressionist art is *Street, Berlin*, painted by Kirchner in 1913.

Meanwhile, in Munich, another Expressionist group called the "Blue Rider" displayed a style characterized by bold heavy outlines, vivid colors and naive features. *The Large Blue Horses* by Franz Marc is a good example of this style of Expressionism.

 Die Kunst ist lang, das Leben kurz.   Art is long but life is short.

The Young Hare
(water color, 1502)
by Albrecht Dürer

Kunstverlag M.u.D. Reisser, Wien

Saint Anthony
(copper engraving, 1519)
by Albrecht Dürer

Staatliche Graphische Sammlung, München

The Large Blue Horses
(oil on canvas, 1911)
by Franz Marc

Collection, Walker Art Center, Minneapolis;
Gift of the T.B. Walker Foundation,
Gilbert M. Walker Fund, 1942

Street, Berlin
(oil on canvas, 1913)
by Ernst Ludwig Kirchner
Collection, The Museum of Modern Art, New York Purchase.

Ships in the Harbor of Greifswald
(oil on canvas, before 1810)
by Caspar David Friedrich
Staatliche Museen Preußischer
Kulturbesitz, Nationalgalerie, Berlin (West)

Lone Tree
(oil on canvas, 1823)
by Caspar David Friedrich
Staatliche Museen Preußischer
Kulturbesitz, Nationalgalerie, Berlin (West)

Exercises

A Name the picture which shows

1. a shepherd leaning against a tree. _____

2. a medieval city. _____

3. an animal at rest. _____

4. animals "moving." _____

5. working people. _____

6. well-dressed city people. _____

B Name the German artist whose works reveal:

1. heavy dark outlines _____

2. exact proportions _____

3. peaceful landscapes _____

4. disturbing elements of nature _____

5. bright colors _____

6. real-looking people or animals _____

C Verbinde B mit A!

A	B
1. Dresden _____	a. Dürer
2. Classical style painter _____	b. where Kirchner studied
3. Nürnberg _____	c. Friedrich
4. Romantic style painter _____	d. where Friedrich lived
5. Expressionist style painter _____	e. Kirchner
6. Greifswald _____	f. where Dürer lived

D Complete the analogies.

1. *Lone Tree*: _____ = *The Four Horsemen*: Dürer

2. Friedrich: seascapes = _____ : city scene

3. Franz Marc: "The Blue Rider" = Kirchner: _____

4. _____ : Classical style = Friedrich: Romantic style

5. _____ : Kirchner = *Saint Anthony*: Dürer

Verbinde den Namen mit der Abbildung!

Friedrich

Kirchner

Dürer

F Which artist would most likely be...

1. awed by dark storm clouds as they rumble across the sky?

   _____

2. happy to write a manual on realism and proportion in art?

   _____

3. disgusted to see an irritated crowd of people at a bus stop?

   _____

G In your opinion...

1. whose work of art would delight a group of Renaissance scholars? _____

2. whose work of art would appeal to someone who likes bright colors and unusual shapes? _____

3. whose work of art would be appreciated by nature-lovers? _____

H Which of the pictures in this unit do you like the best? _____

Who created this masterpiece? _____

State in your own words what the picture is about and why you like it.

_____

_____

_____

_____

_____

I Ergänze die Sätze!

1. Kirchner and Marc were both _____ painters.

2. Friedrich painted many seascapes and _____.

3. Dürer's works are drawn very _____.

Kunst und Kunsthandwerk

Verein für kreatives Gestalten

Kunst-stück e.V.

Bäckerstraße 113   Mo.–Fr. 10–13 Uhr
3380 Goslar   15–18 Uhr
(0 53 21) 2 41 17   Sa. 10–13 Uhr

Puppen & Spielzeug
Museum

8803 Rothenburg ob der Tauber
Hofbronnengasse 13
Telefon (0 98 61) 73 30

Städelsches Kunstinstitut und Städtische Galerie, Schaumainkai 63, ☏ 6 05 09 80
Liebieghaus Museum alter Plastik, Schaumainkai 71, ☏ 21 23 86 17
Museum für Kunsthandwerk, Schaumainkai 71, ☏ 21 23 40 37
Museum für Völkerkunde, Schaumainkai 29, ☏ 21 23 53 90
Historisches Museum, Saalgasse 19, ☏ 21 23 55 99
Kindermuseum, Historisches Museum, Saalgasse 19, ☏ 21 23 51 54
Bundespostmuseum, Schaumainkai 53, ☏ 6 06 01

Naturmuseum Senckenberg,
   Senckenberganlage 25, ☏ 75 42-0
Das Naturmuseum Senckenberg ist das größte seiner Art in der BRD. Besonders sehenswert die riesigen Skelette der Donnerechsen und Saurier.

Goethehaus-Goethemuseum, Großer Hirschgraben 23, ☏ 28 28 24
Struwwelpeter-Museum, Hochstraße 47, ☏ 28 13 33
Museum für Höchster Geschichte und Firmenmuseum der
   Hoechst AG, Höchster Schloß, ☏ 30 32 49
Dommuseum, Am Kaiserdom, ☏ 28 92 29
Frankfurter Feldbahnmuseum, Am Römerhof 15 a, ☏ 70 92 92
Albert Schweitzer Zentrum Archiv und Museum,
Neue Schlesinger Gasse 22-24 (Nähe Alte Oper), ☏ 28 49 51
Deutsches Filmmuseum, Schaumainkai 41, ☏ 21 23 88 30
Deutsches Architektur-Museum, Schaumainkai 43, ☏ 21 23 88 44
Stoltzeturm und Stoltzemuseum, Töngesgasse 34-38, ☏ 21 70 22 66

NEU

Assemblage oder Postmoderne?

Die Kunst unseres Jahrhunderts als reich illustrierte Gesamtschau: Graphik, Objektkunst, Malerei, Fotografie. Auf dem neuesten Stand – hochaktuell. Der kompetente Führer durch die Vielfalt der Kunstrichtungen.

Edward Lucie-Smith beschreibt hier die Ziele und Fakten der modernen Kunst. Er stellt die zeitgenössische Malerei und Plastik in ihren historischen Zusammenhang und gliedert die verwirrende Fülle der internationalen Kunstproduktion unseres Jahrhunderts präzise in Richtungen und Schulen. Dieses einzigartige Werk gibt so eine ausgezeichnete dokumentierte Gesamtschau eines faszinierenden Bereichs unseres kulturellen Lebens.

Ein sensationelles Preis-Leistungs-Verhältnis.
über 750 farbige Abb.
Nur DM 98,-

EDWARD LUCIE-SMITH

DIE MODERNE KUNST

Grafik · Objektkunst · Malerei · Fotografie

SÜDWEST

552 Seiten, 750 farb. Abbildungen.
Großformat 22 x 28 cm.

JA

Wir bestellen hiermit zur umgehenden Lieferung:

____ Expl. DIE GROSSE KUNSTGESCHICHTE DER WELT 98,- DM

____ Expl. DIE MODERNE KUNST 98,- DM

Vorname/Name

in Firma

Straße/Hausnummer

PLZ/Ort

Eigentumsvorbehalt gemäß § 55 BGB.

Humanitas
Buchversand GmbH
Luisenplatz 2
6200 Wiesbaden 1

PARTS OF
THE BODY
Körperteile

der Hals

der Kopf

die Schulter

der
Ellenbogen

die Brust

der Arm

der Bauch

die Hand

das Bein

das Knie

der Fuß

Aus den Augen, aus dem Sinn.   Out of sight, out of mind.

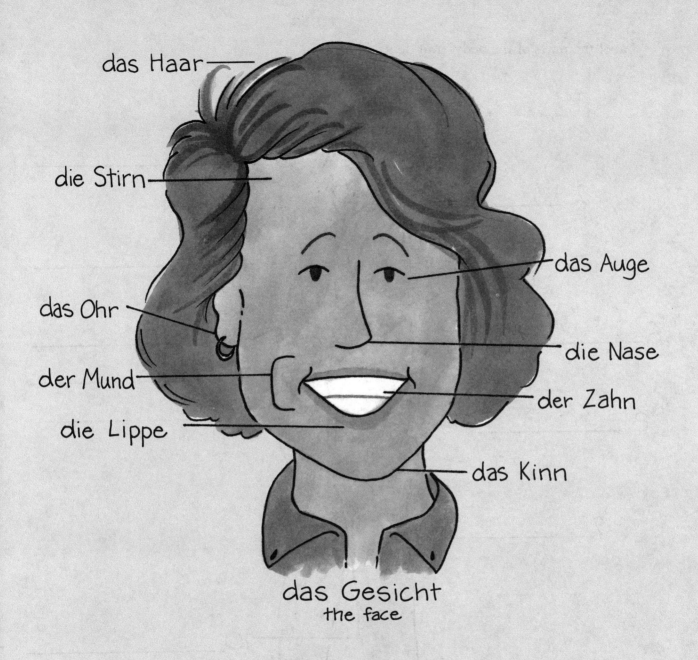

das Haar

die Stirn

das Ohr

der Mund

die Lippe

das Auge

die Nase

der Zahn

das Kinn

das Gesicht
the face

der Finger = the finger	
das Gesicht = the face	
die Zehe = the toe	

die Augen = the eyes	
die Lippen = the lips	
die Ohren = the ears	
die Zähne = the teeth	

Exercises

A Label the parts of the body. (Auf deutsch, bitte.)

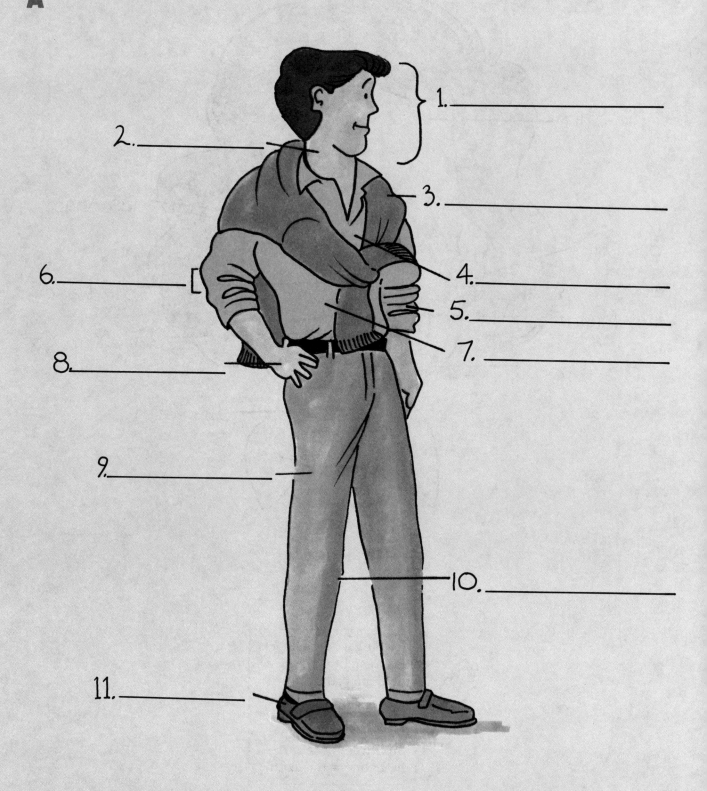

1. _____
2. _____
3. _____
4. _____
5. _____
6. _____
7. _____
8. _____
9. _____
10. _____
11. _____

B   Label the parts of the face. (Auf deutsch, bitte.)

1. _____

2. _____

3. _____

4. _____

5. _____

6. _____

7. _____

8. _____

9. _____

C   Complete the analogies.

1. das Knie: das Bein = _____: der Arm

2. _____: der Fuß = der Arm: das Bein

3. die Finger: _____: die Zehen: der Fuß

D   Ergänze die Sätze auf deutsch!

1. A pirate wears a patch over one _____.

2. The tongue is in the _____.

3. An _____ is necessary for hearing.

4. The pen is held in the _____.

5. _____ are needed to chew food.

6. The toes are found on the _____.

7. We used the _____ to smell a rose.

8. We play a guitar with our _____.

9. The "funny bone" is located on the _____.

10. If you eat too much, your _____ will hurt.

E   Guess the meaning of the underlined verbs.

1. Ich *sehe* mit den Augen. _____

2. Ich *höre* mit den Ohren. _____

3. Ich *fühle* mit den Fingern. _____

4. Ich *spreche* mit dem Mund. _____

5. Ich *rieche* mit der Nase. _____

F Name the part of the body associated with each illustration. (Auf deutsch, bitte.)

1. _____

2. _____

3. _____

4. _____

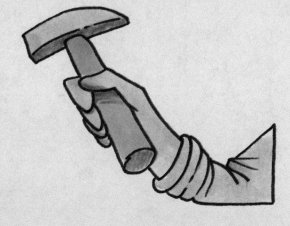

5. _____

6. _____

7. _____

8. _____

9. _____

10. _____

G Verbinde B mit A.

A	B
1. Finger _____	a. smelling
2. Arm _____	b. digesting
3. Bauch _____	c. carrying
4. Nase _____	d. thinking
5. Fuß _____	e. speaking
6. Hand _____	f. listening
7. Auge _____	g. feeling
8. Ohr _____	h. writing
9. Mund _____	i. running
10. Kopf _____	j. seeing

H Lies den Absatz! Wähle die richtigen Antworten!

Ich bin gesund. Ich habe gute Ohren: ich kann gut hören. Ich habe gute Augen: ich kann gut sehen. Ich habe alle Zähne und kann alles essen. Ich habe auch zwei Füße, zwei Beine und zwei Arme. Ich kann gut laufen und schwimmen. Bist du auch gesund?

1. Mein Körper ist...
   a. Ohren   c. gesund
   b. hören   d. zwei

2. Meine Augen sind...
   a. gut   c. Füße
   b. auch   d. sehen

3. Ich esse mit den...
   a. Ohren   c. Augen
   b. Zähnen   d. Beinen

4. Mit den Füßen, Beinen und Armen kann ich...
   a. essen   c. sehen
   b. hören   d. schwimmen

5. Ich bin...
   a. gesund   c. ungesund
   b. laufen   d. essen

Die neuen Gesichter der Deutschen Mark

Annette von Droste-Hülshoff
Poetin mit eigener Note

Damen+Herren Salon Parfümerie

Vermeiden Sie bitte unnötige Wartezeiten!

Lassen Sie sich einen **Termin** geben.

Stüber

Rathausstr. 15 · 2392 Glücksburg
Telefon 0 46 31 / 12 60
Parkplatz hinter dem Haus

Gepflegt durch den Tag!

Theramed Zahncreme
versch. Sorten

jeder 100-ml-Spender **2.⁴⁹**

Fa Duschbad
versch. Sorten

jede 250-ml-Flasche **2.⁷⁹**

Theramed Liquid 2 in 1
versch. Sorten

jede 75-ml-Flasche **3.⁴⁹**

Fa Deo Spray
versch. Sorten

jede 150-ml-Dose **2.⁴⁹**

Fa Schaumbad
versch. Sorten

jede 2-Ltr.-Flasche **9.⁹⁹**

Poly Kur Shampoo
oder **Spülung**
versch. Sorten

jede 250-ml-Flasche **2.⁹⁹**

Fa Seife
versch. Sorten

jedes 125-g-Stück **.79**

CLOTHING
Kleidung

Was hast du an?
Ich habe meine neue Kleidung an.

What are you wearing?
I'm wearing my new clothing.

Lynni
Winterferien
Schweiz — Januar

2 Wollkleider
3 Hüte
1 Schlafanzug
2 Gürtel
3 Taschentücher   3 Hemden
1 Strickjacke   2 Blusen
  Socken
  Handschuhe   Mantel
  Hosen
  Schuhe

Lynni
Winter Vacation
Switzerland — January

2 woolen dresses
3 hats
1 pair of pyjamas
2 belts
3 handkerchiefs   3 shirts
1 cardigan sweater   2 blouses
  socks
  gloves   coat
  pants
  shoes

Moden von Susanne
Oberbekleidung und Unterbekleidung

Bluse

Kleid

Krawatte

Jacke

Bademantel

Anzug

Rock

Pantoffeln

Hemd

Kleider machen Leute.

Clothes make the person.

Exercises

A Verbinde B mit A.

A	B
1. Hüte _____	a. blouse
2. Krawatte _____	b. handkerchief
3. Hemd _____	c. shoes
4. Jacke _____	d. hats
5. Taschentuch _____	e. slippers
6. Bluse _____	f. coat
7. Schuhe _____	g. jacket
8. Pantoffeln _____	h. necktie
9. Mantel _____	i. dress
10. Kleid _____	j. shirt

B What do you wear...(Auf deutsch, bitte.)

1. ˙ to school? _____

2. to bed? _____

3. to a symphony concert? _____

4. in cold weather? _____

5. in cool weather? _____

C Complete the analogies.

1. Krawatte: _____ = Gürtel: Hose

2. Bademantel: Schlafanzug = Mantel: _____

3. Handschuhe: Hände = _____ : Füße

4. _____ : Rock = Hemd: Hose

D Ergänze jeden Satz mit dem Wort für das Bild! *Complete each sentence with the word for the picture.*

1. Ich habe ein _____ an.

2. Ich habe einen _____ an.

3. Ich habe einen _____ an.

4. Ich habe einen _____

   und eine _____ an.

5. Ich habe ein _____

   und eine _____ an.

E Schreib die Wörter auf englisch!

1. anhaben _____

2. er/sie hat an _____

3. ich habe an _____

4. du hast an _____

F Ergänze auf englisch!

1. A "Strickjacke" goes (under/over) a shirt. _____

2. "Schuhe" go over my _____.

3. A "Mantel" is worn when the weather is _____.

4. A "Bluse" is combined with a _____ to make an outfit.

5. "Pantoffeln" go on my _____.

G List the required number of items for each category. (Auf deutsch, bitte.)

outerwear (5)   **accessories (3)**

_____   _____

_____   _____

_____   _____

_____

_____

footwear (3)   **sleepwear (1)**

_____   _____

_____

_____

H Lies den Absatz! Wähle die richtigen Antworten!

Erika geht heute abend mit ihrer Familie ins Konzert. Sie hat ein schönes Kleid an. Da es kalt ist, hat sie auch einen Mantel und Handschuhe an.

1. Wohin (where to) geht Erika heute abend?
   a. mit ihrer Familie
   b. Erika
   c. ins Konzert

2. Was hat Erika an?
   a. ein Kleid
   b. eine Hose
   c. einen Schlafanzug

3. Wie ist das Wetter? (weather)
   a. kalt
   b. warm
   c. kühl

4. Was hat Erika über (over) dem Kleid an?
   a. Handschuhe
   b. einen Mantel
   c. ein Kleid

Kreuzworträtsel

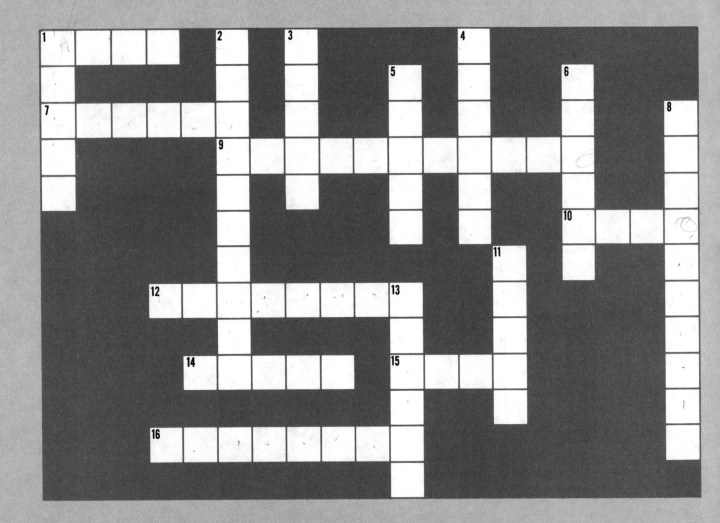

A

Vertical

1. slacks, trousers, pants
2. easily slipped on your feet
3. ...: Rock = Hemd: Hose
4. to wear when it's cold or raining
5. woman: ... = man: Anzug
6. worn on feet outdoors
8. handwarmers
11. worn during cold weather, shorter than coat
13. belts

Horizontal

1. worn on heads
7. put on feet before shoes go on
9. small cloth accessory
10. tie goes on top of...
12. clothing
14. business, leisure, three-piece
15. flared, straight, dirndl
16. must always be worn with a dress shirt

24
Handschuhe
aus Nappaleder
49,95

25
Hut
59,95

26
Schal,
28×150 cm
24,95

27
Ledergürtel
2-St.-Pckg.
24,95

CASHMINK®
SUPERFINE
100% POLYESTER

A B C D

Frotteefuß

BAUMWOLL
STRETCH
Bis
Größe
48

Sortiment B
10 x farbig

2× 2× 2× 2× 2×

3 **Sportsocken** mit Frotteefuß und attraktiven Emblemen. In Weiß: 80% Baumwolle, 20% Polyamid. In Farbe: 65% Baumwolle, 20% Polyamid, 15% Polyacryl. Pflegeleicht. Günstige 10-Paar-Packung.

Schuhgr.	35–38	39–42	43–46	46–48
Sort. A	881.330	881.542	881.660	241.800
Sort. B	984.732	985.632	986.544	987.452
10-Paar-Pckg.	25.-		27.50	

Herren-Flanell-Hemden 12,99
100% Baumwolle · Größen 37–45
hochwertige Superware
39,99/19,99/15,99

Herren-Hemden 10,-
langer Arm · Größen: 37–46
uni u. gestreift, 35% BW

American-T-Shirt 9,99
(Unterzieh-T-Shirt), 100% Baumwolle, Größen: S · M · L · XL
2-Stück-Pack.

PADDOCKS
Schimanski-Jacken 129,99
aus neuester Collektion, lange Form, Größen: S · M · L · XL · XXL, Kapuze unter Reißverschluß, 100% Baumwolle, 4 Aufsatz-Taschen mit Klettverschluß, der Traum eines jeden Mannes – mit dem unvergleichlichen Outfit

LANDROVER
Größe 36–41
69,90

Größe 37–41
59,90

LANDROVER
● gefüttert

Traumhafte Brautmode
zu vernünftigen Preisen!

Brautmoden Goldberg
Marktheidenfeld
Luitpoldpassage
Telefon 09391/81350

Zellingen
Vorstadtstraße 31
Telefon 09364/1552

Lioba-Moden
führt attraktive
Damenmoden
im eleganten und sportlichen Stil ab Größe 38 bis 54 und
Änderungsschneiderei
für Damen und Herren

97828 Marktheidenfeld · Marktplatz 16
Öffnungszeiten: 8.30 bis 17.30 Uhr

1. Stock

ÄNDERUNGS-SCHNEIDEREI
Lioba Moden

FC.
FASHION
COLLECTION
KOMPETENZ IN MODE

MARKT-SONNTAG!

Kommen Sie
von 13.00
bis 18.00 Uhr
zum Mode-Shopping.
Wir nehmen
uns gerne
Zeit für Sie!

MODEHAUS
GRÖN
MARKTHEIDENFELD
MARKTPLATZ

Naturfasern
Handgehäkelte
Details

Holzohr-schmuck
492.352
9.95

1 Pullover
ab
79,90

TIME
AND COLORS
Zeit und Farben

Wieviel Uhr ist es?
Um wieviel Uhr...?

What time is it?
At what time...?

Es ist halb zwei.

Es ist Viertel vor zehn.

Es ist drei Uhr.

Es ist Mittag.

Es ist Viertel nach sieben.

Es ist Mitternacht.

Es ist fünf nach zwei.

Es ist fünf vor zwölf.

> Transportation in Europe operates on official
> time, which has a twenty-four hour basis. Official
> time is often used by schools, radio and television
> stations, theaters and movie theaters.

 Zeit ist Geld.

Time is money.

Welche Farbe hat...?   What color is...?
Es ist...   It is...
Welche Farben haben...? What color are...?
Sie sind...   They are...

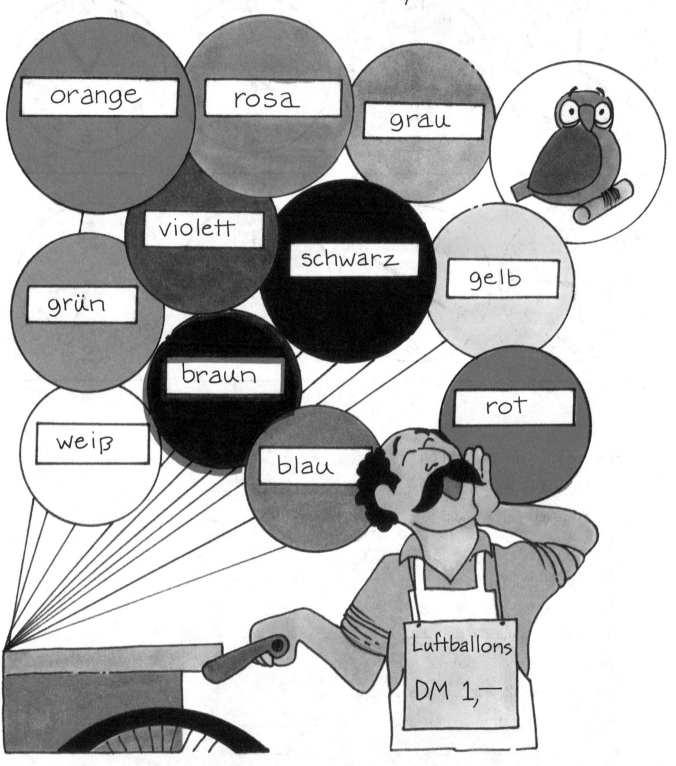

orange

rosa

grau

violett

schwarz

gelb

grün

braun

rot

weiß

blau

Luftballons
DM 1,—

Exercises

A Listen as your teacher indicates a time. Find the clock which expresses that time. Mark the
clock expressing the time said first, number one. Mark the clock expressing the time said
next, number two. Continue numbering until all eight clocks are found and marked.

B Ergänze die Sätze auf deutsch!

1. If the sky is very cloudy, it appears to be _____.

2. If the sky is clear and the sun is shining, the sky is _____.

3. A ripe banana is _____.

4. A leaf in the summer is _____.

5. A piece of coal is _____.

6. A pastel shade of red is _____.

7. A combination of red and yellow is _____.

8. A marshmallow is _____.

9. The color of strawberry is _____.

10. A piece of chocolate is _____.

C Schreib auf deutsch!

1. at four o'clock _____

2. It's half past nine. _____

3. at 12:45 _____

4. It's 10:00. _____

5. at eighteen minutes after two _____

D Welche Farben haben die Objekte?

A		B
1. hearts and tomatoes _____		a. grau
2. frogs and grass _____		b. blau
3. lemons and corn _____		c. grün
4. elephants and rain clouds _____		d. rot
5. forget-me-nots and robins' eggs _____		e. gelb

E Lies den Absatz! Wähle die richtigen Antworten!

Karin und Rolf gehen heute abend ins Konzert. Das Orchester heißt die Berliner Philharmonie. Karin hat ein gelbes Kleid an. Rolfs Anzug ist schwarz, sein Hemd ist rosa und seine Krawatte ist grau und rosa. Die Musik beginnt um 20.00 Uhr. Es ist erst 18.00 Uhr. Die jungen Leute haben zwei Stunden Zeit, bis das Konzert beginnt.

heute abend = this evening	Stunden = hours
jetzt = now	bis = until
die…Leute = the…people	

1. Was ist der Name des Orchesters?
   - a. Karin und Rolf
   - b. Berliner Philharmonie
   - c. Musik
   - d. Konzert

2. Welche Farbe hat Karins Kleid?
   - a. rosa
   - b. weiß
   - c. schwarz
   - d. gelb

3. Paßt Rolfs Krawatte zu seinem Anzug? (Paßt = Does…match)
   - a. ja
   - b. nein

4. Wieviel Uhr ist es jetzt?
   - a. 16.00 Uhr
   - b. 18.00 Uhr
   - c. 20.00 Uhr
   - d. 22.00 Uhr

5. Um wieviel Uhr beginnt das Konzert?
   - a. jetzt
   - b. heute abend
   - c. um 20.00 Uhr
   - d. um 18.00 Uhr

Es ist 3 Uhr.

F   Color the clock according to the directions.

1. Color the "Augen" BRAUN.
2. Color the "Lippen" ROT.
3. Color the "Nase" BLAU.
4. Color the "Haar" VIOLETT
5. Color the "Gesicht" GRAU.
6. Color the "Füße" ROSA.

7. Color the "fünf" GRÜN.
8. Color the "zehn" ORANGE.
9. Color the "elf" SCHWARZ.
10. Color the U GELB.
11. Color the E BLAU.
12. Color the t WEISS.

Wann fährt mein Zug?
Richtung Hamburg

1.09	Hamburg Altona
4.51	Hamburg Harburg
4.54	Hamburg Harburg
5.19	Hamburg Hbf.
5.45	Hamburg Altona
5.48	Hamburg Hbf.
5.57	Hamburg Altona
6.01	Hamburg Harburg
6.02	Hamburg Dammtor
6.24	Hamburg Altona
6.40	Hamburg Harburg
6.43	Hamburg Altona
6.47	Hamburg Dammtor
7.02	Hamburg Dammtor
7.45	Hamburg Altona
7.48	Hamburg Altona
7.58	Hamburg Altona
8.02	Hamburg Hbf.
8.10	Hamburg Hbf.
8.42	Hamburg Altona
8.59	Hamburg Altona
9.22	Hamburg Harburg
9.58	Hamburg Altona
11.20	Hamburg Altona
11.58	Hamburg Altona
12.38	Hamburg Dammtor
12.41	Hamburg Harburg
12.52	Hamburg Harburg
13.17	Hamburg Harburg
13.38	Hamburg Harburg
13.47	Hamburg Harburg
13.58	Hamburg Altona
14.38	Hamburg Dammtor

ZUM AUFZIEHEN

FRECHE **F**ARBEN **M**ACHEN **S**PASS!

1 Je 19.95 In mehreren Farben

2 Je 29.95

MEISTER-ANKER

4 Wasserdicht Je 29.95

3 Je 25.–

6 Kinderuhren mit Quarzwerk je 25.–

5 Wasserdicht Je 39.95

Kein 'Aufziehen mehr!

uhren müller

die weitbekannte Adresse an der Mosel mit der besonderen Note

5590 COCHEM - BERNSTRASSE 5 TEL. 02671/8402

Luxus walk

blau
gelb
rot
mint
flieder
apricot

altrosa
bordeaux
weiß
grün
natur
lila

3 Handtücher
2 Stück Packung
27⁹⁵

Das
Info-Büro

Telefon: 0551/400-4444

Öffnungszeiten:
Montag–Mittwoch   7.30 – 16.00 Uhr
Donnerstag   7.30 – 17.30 Uhr
Freitag   7.30 – 14.00 Uhr

Antik: Sonntag, 13 Uhr geht's los
die Riesen-Verkaufs-Fete beim Al-tertümer-Riesen; ca. 500 Stühle und Tische, Hunderte von Möbeln und Tausende von Kleinteilen! Ihr Kommen lohnt sich allemal!
Antik-Handel-Schmelz
Marktheidenfeld (a.d. Brücke)

14

MUSIC
Musik

Three Great Musicians

Johann Sebastian Bach (1685–1750) was born in Eisenach. Orphaned at the age of ten and raised by his brother, young Bach was a gifted musician who became a master of the organ, the harpsichord and the violin. He wrote hundreds of musical compositions. His music includes church music as well as compositions for specific instruments and groups of instruments. Bach's last and longest employment was as organist and choir teacher at the Church of St. Thomas in Leipzig. Today, he is considered the father of Baroque music. He married twice and was the father of twenty children. A year before his death Bach became totally blind. The *Brandenburg Concertos*, *The Well-Tempered Clavier* and the *Christmas Oratorio* are three of his many famous works.

Wolfgang Amadeus Mozart (1756–1791) was born in Salzburg, Austria. He was educated by his father, an accomplished musician, and was writing minuets at the age of five. At six, Mozart performed as a child prodigy for the royal courts of Europe.

Mozart is the finest representative of the Classical period of music. His fame resided in his ability to learn, reproduce from memory and create masterpieces effortlessly.

He wrote operas, symphonies, chamber music and church music. In spite of his superb talent and musical genius, Mozart never earned enough to support his wife and children. He died at the age of thirty-five and was buried in a pauper's grave. His masterpieces include *Eine Kleine Nachtmusik* (chamber music), *The Magic Flute* (opera) and the *Jupiter Symphony*.

Ludwig van Beethoven (1770–1827) was born in Bonn, then a small village on the Rhine River. He was introduced to music at an early age and soon became an organist at the Elector's court in Bonn. Beethoven left his home in Bonn to study in Vienna, the musical capital of Europe at the time. Although recalled to Bonn by family problems, he did return to Vienna to study under Haydn. Beethoven became interested in the democratic ideals of the French Revolution and in the Romantics' view of nature and beauty. He often reflected these interests in his music. His opera *Fidelio* and his *Fifth* and *Sixth Symphonies* are good examples of these interests.

In Vienna the composer soon became an established musician. In spite of his international fame, Beethoven had to suffer many personal tragedies. His last twelve years were spent in total deafness. Beethoven is acclaimed today as the greatest composer of the Romantic era.

Sie spielt die erste Geige.　　　　She plays the first fiddle.

Exercises

A Give the full name and the dates of the composer who:

1. could effortlessly memorize and play musical compositions. _____

2. composed mainly for church services and individual instruments. _____

3. started his career as an organist at the Elector's court. _____

B Verbinde B mit A.

A	B
1. *Jupiter Symphony* _____	a. symphony by Beethoven
2. *Brandenburg Concertos* _____	b. home of Bach
3. *Fifth Symphony* _____	c. symphony by Mozart
4. Salzburg _____	d. instrumental works by Bach
5. Leipzig _____	e. birthplace of Mozart

C Guess who...

1. was a child prodigy. _____

2. was a pupil of Haydn. _____

3. wrote pieces for the harpsichord and organ. _____

4. became deaf. _____

5. became blind. _____

D Complete the analogies.

1. Ludwig: van Beethoven = _____ : Bach

2. *The Well-Tempered Clavier*: _____ = *Eine Kleine Nachtmusik*: Mozart

3. _____ : Beethoven = *The Magic Flute*: Mozart

4. Bach: Eisenach = Mozart: _____

5. harpsichord music: Bach = minuets: _____

E Verbinde B mit A.

A	B
1. Bach _____	a. Romantic music
2. Mozart _____	b. Baroque music
3. Beethoven _____	c. Classical music

Verbinde den Namen mit der Abbildung!

Mozart

Bach

Beethoven

G Schreib die Namen richtig.

1. HACB _____

2. HOBNEETVE _____

3. TARZOM _____

4. SUEDAAM _____

5. NNOHJA _____

Kreuzworträtsel

H

Vertical

1. birthplace of Beethoven
2. Beethoven's kind of music
3. birthplace of Bach
4. Mozart was a child. . . .
5. birthplace of Mozart
6. Bach's *Brandenburg* . . . .

Horizontal

1. Bach's kind of music
6. Mozart's kind of music
7. Beethoven's first name
8. a Mozart symphony

OPER FRANKFURT

Untermeinanlage 11, 60311 Frankfurt, Telefon 069 / 2 12 02

03.10.	**Jeder Mensch ist ein Abgrund**, eine literaisch-musikalische Matinee zu Wozzeck, Holzfoyer	11.00 Uhr
06.+08.10.	**Wozzeck** Oper von Alban Berg (am 06. Premiere)	20.00 Uhr
09.10.	**Ballettabend** Ballette von William Forsythe	20.00 Uhr
10.10.	**Quintette mit Kontrabass** Kammermusik im Foyer 1	11.00 Uhr
	Wozzeck Oper von Alban Berg	20.00 Uhr
13.10.	**Ballettabend** Ballette von William Forsythe	20.00 Uhr
14.10.	**Wozzeck** Oper von Alban Berg	20.00 Uhr
15.10.	**Ballettabend** Ballette von William Forsythe	20.00 Uhr
16.10.	Wiederaufnahme: **Il Barbiere di Siviglia**	19.30 Uhr
17.10.	**Wozzeck** Oper von Alban Berg	20.00 Uhr
19.10.	**Happy new ears 1** Ensemble Modern	20.30 Uhr
20.10.	**Wozzeck** Oper von Alban Berg	20.00 Uhr
23.10.	**Il Barbiere di Siviglia** Oper von Gioacchino Rossini	19.30 Uhr
24.10.	**Wozzeck** Oper von Alban Berg	20.00 Uhr
25.10.	Wiederaufnahme: **Cosi fan Tutte**	19.30 Uhr
27.10.	**Wozzeck** Oper von Alban Berg	20.00 Uhr
28.10.	**Cosi fan Tutte**	19.30 Uhr
29.10.	**Il Barbiere di Siviglia** Oper von Gioacchino Rossini	19.30 Uhr
30.10.	**Cosi fan Tutte** Oper von Wolfgang Amadeus Mozart	19.30 Uhr
31.10.	**Wozzeck** Oper von Alban Berg	15.30 Uhr

ENTERTAINMENT

»Phantom of the Opera«
PETER HOFMANN
ANNA MARIA KAUFMANN
singen
MUSICAL CLASSICS
PHANTOM DER OPER.
WEST SIDE STORY. CATS u.v.a.
begleitet von 50 Mitgliedern des
NDR-Sinfonieorchester
unter der Leitung von Carl Robert Helg.
12.10. FRANKFURT · FESTHALLE Frankfurt

Göttinger Meister Konzerte

Theater & Konzerte

Theater der Stadt Duisburg
MARGARETE
11. Oktober   19:30 Uhr
II. Rang Mitte rechts
Reihe 1   Platz 26
                    DM 17.00
01-8810114-22/001/0026-01e-22

Duisburg

NIKOLAIKIRCHE ZU LEIPZIG

ORGELKONZERT

Juli / August
Mittwoch, 20.00 Uhr

Eintritt: DM 5,–
unnumerierter Platz   Nr   122

Karte gilt für eine Veranstaltung

»Hier ist der Ruhepunkt der Woche«

Gewandhaus zu Leipzig

Gewandhauskonzerte

Dienstagskonzerte · Orgelkonzerte

Kammermusik

GEWANDHAUS LEIPZIG
Augustusplatz 8 · O-7010 Leipzig
Telefon 7 13 20 · Fax 7 13 22 00
Kartenbestellung, Vorverkauf sowie Informationen zum
Anrechtserwerb an der Gewandhauskasse
Telefon 77 96 und 7 18 00
Öffnungszeiten Mo. 11–16 Uhr, Die. bis Fr. 11–17
und Abendkasse 1 Stunde vor Konzertbeginn

JAZZ STUDIO   ● Paniersplatz 27/29

04.	FERDINAND HAVLIK SEXTET	20.00
05.	JOE SACHSE - Solo	20.00
06.	SWINGIN CLARINETS mit Walter Schätzlein	20.00
11.	SWINGIN BEBOP, BARBARA DENNERLEIN TRIO	20.00
12.	DUSKO STRAIGHT AHEAD. GOYKOVICH & H.	20.00
13.	CD - REVIEW mit Manfred Mangold	20.00
18.	FROM BOP TO FREE: CROSS TALK FEAT	20.00
19.	VOCAL JAZZ. ÖZAY TRIO FEAT JIM PEPPER	20.00
20.	JAZZMAGAZIN mit Walter Schätzlein	20.00
25.	THE ART OF DUO. KAGERER - NIEBERLE	20.00
26.	BALLROOM JAZZ, K.B. JUNGLE BAND	20.00
27.	JAZZ TRIBUTE TO THE BEATLES mit A. Mangold	20.00

15

WEATHER AND SEASONS
Wetter und Jahreszeiten

Wie ist das Wetter?   How's the weather?

Es ist schön.   So, so.   Es ist schlecht.

Es ist sonnig.	It's sunny.	Es ist kühl.	It's cool.	Es ist kalt.	It's cold.
Es ist warm.	It's warm.	Es ist windig.	It's windy.	Es blitzt.	It's lightning.
Es ist heiß.	It's hot.	Es ist schwül.	It's humid.	Es schneit.	It's snowing.
		Es ist wolkig.	It's cloudy.	Es donnert.	It's thundering.
				Es regnet.	It's raining.

Welche Jahreszeit haben wir?   What's the season?
Wir haben . . .   It's . . .

Die vier Jahreszeiten

der Frühling

der Herbst

der Winter

der Sommer

 Use "im" before a season:
"im Sommer" = in the summer

 Der April macht die Blumen,   April showers
und der Mai hat den Dank dafür.   bring May flowers.

A   Verbinde den Satz mit der Abbildung!

1. _____   a. Es ist sonnig.

2. _____   b. Es blitzt.

3. _____   c. Es regnet.

4. _____   d. Es ist windig.

5. _____   e. Es ist kalt.

B Wie ist das Wetter? Beantworte die Frage auf deutsch!

1. _____

2. _____

3. _____

4. _____

5. _____

C Verbinde die Jahreszeit mit der Abbildung!

1. _____ a. Sommer

2. _____ b. Winter

3. _____ c. Frühling

4. _____ d. Herbst

D Write in column one the English for each word at the left. When you have finished the entire column, cover the column of words at the left, and in column two, write the English words in German.

column one

(English)

column two

(German)

		column one	column two
1.	Sonne	1._____	1._____
2.	Blitz	2._____	2._____
3.	Frühling	3._____	3._____
4.	Sommer	4._____	4._____
5.	Wetter	5._____	5._____
6.	Herbst	6._____	6._____
7.	Jahreszeit	7._____	7._____
8.	kühl	8._____	8._____
9.	heiß	9._____	9._____
10.	Es regnet.	10._____	10._____
11.	Winter	11._____	11._____
12.	schlecht	12._____	12._____
13.	Donner	13._____	13._____
14.	kalt	14._____	14._____

E Verbinde B mit A.

A

nouns

B

verbs

	A		B
1.	Regen _____	a.	donnern
2.	Schnee _____	b.	schneien
3.	Donner _____	c.	regnen
4.	Blitz _____	d.	scheinen
5.	Sonne _____	e.	blitzen

F Wie ist das Wetter? (Auf deutsch, bitte.) *Using the cue at the left, write a statement about the weather.*

1. mittens and parka _____

2. sunglasses _____

3. lightning bolts _____

4. cardigan sweater _____

5. outdoor tennis court _____

6. umbrella _____

7. snowflakes _____

8. air conditioner _____

9. sailboat _____

10. rain, wind and hail _____

G Lies den Absatz und dann wähle die richtigen Antworten!

Die vier Jahreszeiten

Im Winter ist es sehr kalt und es schneit oft. Der Schnee ist weiß. Im Frühling ist es windig, kühl und regnerisch. Das Wetter im Sommer ist sonnig und heiß. Im Herbst ist es wieder kühl und windig. Die vier Jahreszeiten sind wunderbar.

1. Wie viele Jahreszeiten gibt es?
   a. eine
   b. vier
   c. zwei
   d. drei

2. Wie ist das Wetter im Winter?
   a. Es ist Winter.
   b. Es ist schön.
   c. Es ist warm.
   d. Es ist kalt.

3. Im Frühling ist es....
   a. regnerisch
   b. heiß
   c. kalt
   d. weiß

4. Die Sonne scheint viel im....
   a. Sommer
   b. Herbst
   c. Frühling
   d. Winter

Kreuzworträtsel

H

Vertical

2. When water runs off a duck's back, "es..."
3. When dazzling streaks illuminate the sky, "es..."
5. season of floral rebirth
6. harvest season (temperate zone)
7. skiing season
9. hazy, hot and muggy
11. not very "kalt"
13. "Es regnet...Herbst."

Horizontal

1. Dinner rolls should be served...
4. A hazy day is...
7. what everyone talks about
8. Winter is a...(of four seasons)
9. very nice out
10. time for picnics and swimming
11. Ice cubes are...
12. March is traditionally...
14. normal summer temperature (ß = ss)

Reisewetter

Norddeutschland: Im Südosten regnerisch, sonst wechselnd bewölkt und wiederholt Schauer. Deutlich kühler mit Höchsttemperaturen zwischen 10 und 15 Grad.

Schweden: Wechselnd bewölkt. Zeitweise Regen, im Norden und in höheren Lagen Schneefall. Im äußersten Süden anfangs noch bei 10 Grad, sonst 1 bis 6 Grad.

Norwegen: Wechsel zwischen aufgelockerter und starker Bewölkung. Wiederholt Regen, im Norden und in höheren Lagen Schneefall. 1 bis 6 Grad.

Dänemark: Wechselnd bewölkt mit einzelnen Schauern. Nur noch um 8 Grad. Später freundlicher, aber sehr kühl.

Finnland: Teils aufgelockerte teils starke Bewölkung, zeitweise Regen. 4 bis 9 Grad. Später nur noch zwischen plus 3 und minus 2 Grad, dabei im Norden zeitweise Schneefall.

Benelux und Nordfrankreich: Länger andauernder Regen bei 14 Grad. Zurückgehende Temperaturen.

Großbritannien/Irland: Bei wechselnder Bewölkung treten einzelne Schauer auf. Die Temperaturen liegen bei 10, im Norden nur bei 6 Grad.

Temperaturen

Angaben vom Vortag, 14 Uhr

Inland
Berlin, Regen, 10°
Dresden, Regen, 18°
Freiburg, wolkig, 17°
Hamburg, Regen, 9°

Köln-Bonn, stark bewölkt, 14°
München, Regen, 13°
Nürnberg, stark bewölkt, 14°
Passau, Regen, 15°

Ausland
Amsterdam, Regen, 9°
Athen, leicht bewölkt, 26°
Istanbul, wolkenlos, 24°
Kopenhagen, Regen, 5°

Las Palmas, wolkig, 23°
Lissabon, wolkig, 23°
London, leicht bewölkt, 11°
Mallorca, leicht bewölkt, 21°
Moskau, leicht bewölkt, 17°
Nizza, leicht bewölkt, 20°
Paris, Regen, 14°
Prag, stark bewölkt, 18°
Rom, bedeckt, 24°
Stockholm, leicht bewölkt, 6°

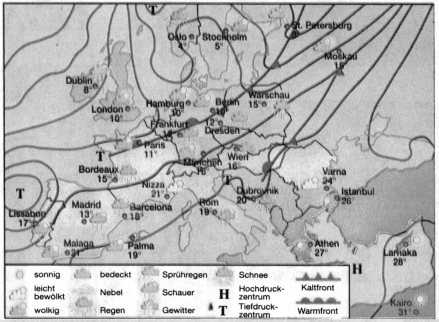

○ sonnig	bedeckt	Sprühregen	Schnee	Kaltfront
leicht bewölkt	Nebel	Schauer	**H** Hochdruckzentrum	Warmfront
wolkig	Regen	Gewitter	**T** Tiefdruckzentrum	

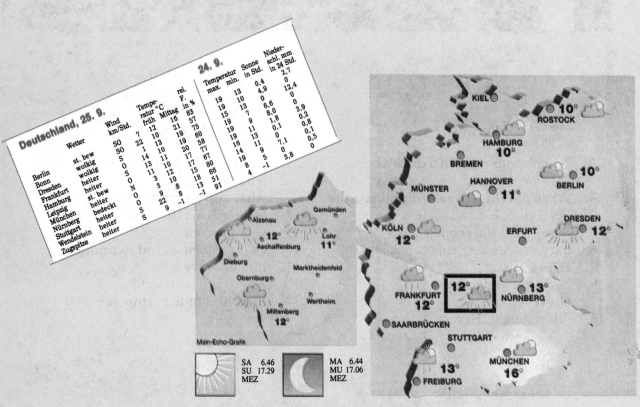

Deutschland, 25. 9.

	Wetter	Wind km/Std.	Temperatur °C früh	Temperatur °C Mittag	rel. F. in %			Temperatur max.	Temperatur min.	Sonne in Std.	Niederschl. mm in 24 Std.
						24. 9.					2,7
Berlin	st. bew	SO	7	12	83			19	13	0,4	0
Bonn	wolkig	SO	22	16	57			19	10	4,9	12,4
Dresden	wolkig	S	10	21	75			15	13	6,6	0
Frankfurt	heiter	S	14	19	60			19	7	8,0	3,9
Hamburg	heiter	S	11	20	58			19	9	1,8	0,2
Leipzig	st. bew	O	11	17	67			19	11	0,1	0,8
München	bedeckt	N	13	12	80			19	13	0	0,1
Nürnberg	heiter	O	3	10	51			16	11	7,1	0,5
Stuttgart	heiter	O	9	12	66			14	9		0
Wendelstein	heiter	S	9	8	91			19	5	3,8	
Zugspitze	heiter		22	-1				8	-1		

Main-Echo-Grafik

SA 6.46
SU 17.29
MEZ

MA 6.44
MU 17.06
MEZ

16

DAYS AND MONTHS
Tage und Monate

Welcher Tag ist heute ?
Heute ist...

What day is today?
Today is...

Monday Montag	Dienstag	Mittwoch	Donnerstag	Freitag	Samstag (Sonnabend)	Sonntag
	1	2	3	4	5	6
7	8	9	10	11	12	13
14	15	16	17	18	19	20
21	22	23	24	25	26	27
28	29	30	31			

Welches Datum haben wir?
Heute ist der erste Mai.

What is the date today?
It's May first today.

April
Mai
Juni

Oktober
November
Dezember

Januar
Februar
März

Juli
August
September

Morgen, morgen, nur nicht
heute, sagen alle faulen Leute.

Don't put off until tomorrow
what you can do today.

Derivations and Comparisons

German Day	Norse Mythology
Montag	day honoring the moon god "Mond" = moon
Dienstag	day honoring Tyr, a Norse god of war, and/or Mars Thingsus, the Roman god of war The latter was also known as God of the Assembly and Protector of the Tribal Councils. "Dienstag" was Tribal Council Day.
Mittwoch	day honoring Wodan or Odin, father of the gods and a god of war Wodan's Day = Wednesday Wodan often wore a hat with a wide brim and carried a large staff. The Romans compared him to Mercury with his caduseus or staff.
Donnerstag	day honoring Thor, god of weather and thunder, and son of Wodan Thor = Donner = thunder Thor's Day = Thursday Thor always carried an enormous hammer. The Romans found him similar to Hercules and his club.
Freitag	day honoring Freia, goddess of love, and wife of Wodan. The Romans compared her to their goddess Venus.
Samstag	day honoring Saturn, Roman god of the harvest and agriculture
Sonntag	day honoring the sun god "Sonne" = sun

Jakobs Heft

Lerne für die Englischarbeit!

1. tomorrow   (mein Geburtstag)
2. the day after tomorrow
3. yesterday
4. the day before yesterday
5. the day
6. the holiday   (Bravo!)
7. the school day   (Mensch!)
8. the birthday   (morgen)
9. the week
10. the weekend   (mein Leben)
11. the month

Jakob's Notebook

Learn for English test:

1. morgen
2. übermorgen
3. gestern
4. vorgestern
5. der Tag
6. der Feiertag
7. der Schultag
8. der Geburtstag
9. die Woche
10. das Wochenende
11. der Monat

Exercises

A Write in numerical form the dates which your teacher reads.

1. _____

2. _____

3. _____

4. _____

5. _____

B Label the current month. Include the names of the days and all the numbers.

MONAT _____

TAG	TAG	TAG	TAG	TAG	TAG	TAG

C Schreib die Daten!

1. Wednesday, December 25th _____

2. Saturday, November 11th _____

3. Thursday, May 1st _____

4. Sunday, June 17th _____

5. Monday, April 19th _____

D Complete the following in English.

1. If the date is 9.1.95 (German date), what is the month?

_____

2. What happens when Thor, the weathergod, strikes his hammer? Explain what you hear.

_____

3. Identify the family of gods represented in the weekdays.

mother _____

father _____

son _____

E Verbinde B mit A.

A	B
1. übermorgen _____	a. tomorrow
2. heute _____	b. yesterday
3. morgen _____	c. day before yesterday
4. vorgestern _____	d. day after tomorrow
5. gestern _____	e. today

F Schreib auf deutsch!

1. the day after "Mittwoch" _____

2. the two summer vacation months _____

3. the day that was "vorgestern" _____

4. the "Monat" that begins the calendar year _____

5. the day that is "morgen" _____

6. your favorite day _____

7. your garbage collection day _____

8. your "Geburtstag" month _____

G Schreib den deutschen Tag der Abbildung nach!

1. _____

2. _____

3. _____

4. _____

5.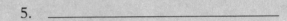

6. _____

7. _____

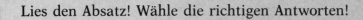

H Lies den Absatz! Wähle die richtigen Antworten!

Heute ist Freitag und das ist fantastisch. Das Wochenende kommt. Am Samstag ist ein Fußballspiel. Die deutsche Mannschaft spielt gegen Frankreich. Meine Freunde und ich interessieren uns sehr für Fußball. Wir spielen sehr oft Fußball. Sonntag ist Familientag. Ich gehe am Sonntag mit meiner Familie spazieren. Wir sprechen oft über Fußball, das Wetter, die Schule und die kommende Woche. Das Wochenende ist bald da!

der Fußball	soccer
das Spiel	game
die Mannschaft	team
spielen	to play
gegen	against
spazieren	(to go) walking
sprechen	to speak
bald	soon

1. Warum ist Freitag fantastisch?
   a. Das Wetter ist schön.   c. Ich spreche über Fußball.
   b. Heute ist Freitag.   d. Das Wochenende kommt.

2. Wann ist das Fußballspiel?
   a. am Freitag   c. am Sonntag
   b. am Samstag   d. am Montag

3. Ist Fußball mein Hobby?
   a. ja   b. nein

4. Was mache ich am Sonntag?
   a. Ich gehe spazieren.   c. Ich gehe in die Schule.
   b. Ich spiele Fußball.   d. Ich interessiere mich für Fußball.

5. Wer geht mit mir spazieren?
   a. mein Fußball   c. meine Familie
   b. mein Fisch   d. meine Freunde

Kreuzworträtsel

Vertical

1. birthmonth of Washington and Lincoln
2. day honoring the goddess of love
4. month of American independence
5. One attends classes on a...
6. from Friday afternoon until Sunday evening
7. noisy day of the week
9. opposite of "Abend"
10. moonday
11. date
14. "dog days" month

Horizontal

3. "gestern,...und morgen"
4. month of the year's first holiday
8. month in which summer begins
9. day in the middle of the week
10. month of Martians
12. Today is the tomorrow worried about...
13. day honoring the god of heat and light
15. "Guten...."
16. a weekend day
17. the most necessary day in a person's life

Horoskop

Donnerstag,
14. Oktober

Wenn Sie heute Geburtstag haben:

Sie müssen sich im nächsten Jahr auf unerwartete und spontane Veränderungen einstellen. Mit Geduld und Disziplin können Sie daraus Kapital schlagen. Auch der Liebe sollten Sie die Zeit lassen, die sie braucht. Lassen Sie sich nicht von Streß und Hektik überollen – sonst drohen gesundheitliche Rückschläge.

WIDDER
(21. 3.–20. 4.): Sie fühlen sich eingeengt. Besonders von Ihrem Partner. Es ist nur eine Frage der Zeit, bis Sie ausbrechen. Doch denken Sie bei aller Versuchung daran: Gesundheit: Sie sind zur Zeit etwas anfällig für Infektionen. Viel frisches Obst hilft.
☎ 0190/24 23 01

STIER
(21. 4.–20. 5.): Nicht jeder denkt so schnell wie Sie. Seien Sie deshalb nicht gleich eingeschnappt, wenn andere nicht Ihrer Meinung sind. Ihre erotischen Phantasien bleiben – leider – für eine Weile noch ein Traum. Achten Sie in nächster Zeit mehr auf Ihren Magen.
☎ 0190/24 23 02

ZWILLINGE
(21. 5.–21. 6.): Bei aller Power, die in Ihnen steckt – halten Sie sich im Augenblick besser zurück. So könnten sich auch Spannungen in der Partnerschaft entkrampfen. Gesundheitlich alles o. k. Gute Zeit für Bewerbungsschreiben.
☎ 0190/24 23 03

KREBS
(22. 6.–22. 7.): Hindernisse sind da, um gemeistert zu werden. Trotz-dem Vorsicht: leichte Unfallgefahr. Seien Sie in der Liebe nicht zu dickschädelig. Ihr Partner könnte es auf eine Machtprobe ankommen lassen – die Sie verlieren.
☎ 0190/24 23 04

LÖWE
(23. 7.–23. 8.): Hand auf den Geldbeutel, jemand spekuliert auf Ihre Großzügigkeit. Er heuchelt aber nur Freundschaft vor. Verlassen Sie sich am besten auf den Menschen, der Sie liebt. Treten Sie etwas kürzer. Sie sind nämlich längst nicht so fit, wie Sie glauben.
☎ 0190/24 23 05

JUNGFRAU
(24. 8.–23. 9.): Jetzt zahlt es sich aus, daß Sie die ganze Zeit so fair und gerecht waren. Sie haben bei anderen großes Vertrauen gewonnen. Ihr neues Selbstbewußtsein stärkt auch Ihren Körper und strahlt harmonisch auf Ihr Liebesleben aus.
☎ 0190/24 23 06

WAAGE
(24. 9.–23. 10.): Sehen Sie vielleicht manches im Augenblick zu sehr durch die rosarote Brille? Weit-reichende Entscheidungen sollten Sie momentan besser zurückstellen.
Ihr Partner wartet auf ein offenes Wort. Achtung: Grippegefahr!
☎ 0190/24 23 07

SKORPION
(24. 10.–22. 11.): So sehr es Sie auch juckt – halten Sie sich aus allen Machtkämpfen am Arbeitsplatz heraus. Investieren Sie Ihr Gespür für Menschen lieber in einen Flirt. Die Chancen stehen nicht schlecht. Nehmen Sie Kopfschmerzen nicht auf die leichte Schulter.
☎ 0190/24 23 08

SCHÜTZE
(23. 11.–21. 12.): Werden Sie nicht leichtsinnig. Im Moment haben Sie kein Händchen für Glücksspiele. Aber wie heißt es: Pech im Spiel – Glück in der Liebe. Überwinden Sie Ihre Trägheit, Ihr Körper braucht ein bißchen Aufbautraining.
☎ 0190/24 23 09

STEINBOCK
(22. 12.–20. 1.): Leise tickt eine Bombe unter der Oberfläche Ihrer Liebesbeziehung . . . Entschärfen Sie sie, ehe es zur Explosion kommt. Ein Kollege zeigt plötzlich sein wahres Gesicht. Das feuchtnasse Herbstwetter könnte Ihren Gelenken zu schaffen machen.
☎ 0190/24 23 10

WASSERMANN
(21. 1.–20. 2.): Ein Mensch in Ihrer Umgebung wartet drauf, daß Sie ihm aus der Patsche helfen. Sie haben die Kraft dazu. Als Belohnung wartet auf Sie ein besonders schöner Schmuse-Abend. Aber Vorsicht vor zuviel Alkohol, besonders scharfe Sachen meiden. ☎ 0190/24 23 11

FISCHE
(21. 2.–20. 3.): Ihre Erfolgskurve zeigt weiter steil nach oben. Doch der Gipfel ist fast erreicht, und dahinter lauern Neider. In der Partnerschaft finden Sie die zärtliche Geborgenheit, die Sie jetzt brauchen. Gesundheit: verstärkte Anfälligkeit für Allergien und Hautreizungen.
☎ 0190/24 23 12

Das Wetter für die ganze Woche

Montag	Dienstag	Mittwoch	Donnerstag	Freitag	Samstag
12° bis 15°	12° bis 15°	10° bis 13°	9° bis 12°	8° bis 11°	7° bis 10°

	Hochsauerland + Wittgenstein ab. 500 m Monatsdurchschnitt*		Mittl. Sauerl./Siegerl. + Wittgenstein unt. 500 m Monatsdurchschnitt*	
	Temp.	Sonne Std.	Temp.	Sonne Std.
Jan.	− 1	43	− 3	45
Febr.	− 2	68	− 1	65
März	+ 2	115	+ 3	113
April	+ 6	145	+ 7	145
Mai	+10	185	+12	180
Juni	+13	205	+15	200
Juli	+16	195	+15	190
Aug.	+14	155	+16	153
Sept.	+11	145	+13	144
Okt.	+ 7	115	+ 8	115
Nov.	+ 2	43	+ 3	46
Dez.	− 1	40	± 0	40

*Mittelwerte. Die höchsten bzw. niedrigsten Temperaturen wurden hierbei nicht berücksichtigt.
Am „Kahlen Asten" liegen die Durchschnittstemperaturen um ca. 3–5 °Celsius niedriger.

KALENDER

	Januar							Februar							März							April					
Mo		3	10	17	24	31	Mo		7	14	21	28		Mo		7	14	21	28		Mo		4	11	18	25	
Di		4	11	18	25		Di	1	8	15	22			Di	1	8	15	22	29		Di		5	12	19	26		
Mi		5	12	19	26		Mi	2	9	16	23			Mi	2	9	16	23	30		Mi		6	13	20	27		
Do		6	13	20	27		Do	3	10	17	24			Do	3	10	17	24	31		Do		7	14	21	28		
Fr		7	14	21	28		Fr	4	11	18	25			Fr	4	11	18	25			Fr	1	8	15	22	29		
Sa	1	8	15	22	29		Sa	5	12	19	26			Sa	5	12	19	26			Sa	2	9	16	23	30		
So	2	9	16	23	30		So	6	13	20	27			So	6	13	20	27			So	3	10	17	24			

	Mai							Juni							Juli							August					
Mo		2	9	16	23	30	Mo		6	13	20	27		Mo		4	11	18	25		Mo	1	8	15	22	29	
Di		3	10	17	24	31	Di		7	14	21	28		Di		5	12	19	26		Di	2	9	16	23	30	
Mi		4	11	18	25		Mi	1	8	15	22	29		Mi		6	13	20	27		Mi	3	10	17	24	31	
Do		5	12	19	26		Do	2	9	16	23	30		Do		7	14	21	28		Do	4	11	18	25		
Fr		6	13	20	27		Fr	3	10	17	24			Fr	1	8	15	22	29		Fr	5	12	19	26		
Sa		7	14	21	28		Sa	4	11	18	25			Sa	2	9	16	23	30		Sa	6	13	20	27		
So	1	8	15	22	29		So	5	12	19	26			So	3	10	17	24	31		So	7	14	21	28		

	September							Oktober							November							Dezember					
Mo		5	12	19	26		Mo		3	10	17	24	31	Mo		7	14	21	28		Mo		5	12	19	26	
Di		6	13	20	27		Di		4	11	18	25		Di	1	8	15	22	29		Di		6	13	20	27	
Mi		7	14	21	28		Mi		5	12	19	26		Mi	2	9	16	23	30		Mi		7	14	21	28	
Do	1	8	15	22	29		Do		6	13	20	27		Do	3	10	17	24			Do	1	8	15	22	29	
Fr	2	9	16	23	30		Fr		7	14	21	28		Fr	4	11	18	25			Fr	2	9	16	23	30	
Sa	3	10	17	24			Sa	1	8	15	22	29		Sa	5	12	19	26			Sa	3	10	17	24	31	
So	4	11	18	25			So	2	9	16	23	30		So	6	13	20	27			So	4	11	18	25		

Five Great Authors

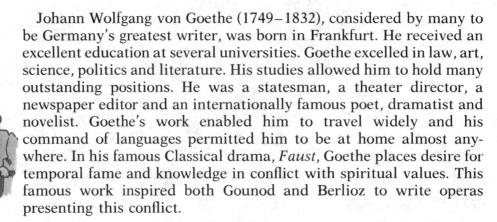

Johann Wolfgang von Goethe (1749–1832), considered by many to be Germany's greatest writer, was born in Frankfurt. He received an excellent education at several universities. Goethe excelled in law, art, science, politics and literature. His studies allowed him to hold many outstanding positions. He was a statesman, a theater director, a newspaper editor and an internationally famous poet, dramatist and novelist. Goethe's work enabled him to travel widely and his command of languages permitted him to be at home almost anywhere. In his famous Classical drama, *Faust*, Goethe places desire for temporal fame and knowledge in conflict with spiritual values. This famous work inspired both Gounod and Berlioz to write operas presenting this conflict.

Friedrich Schiller (1759–1805) was born in the little city of Marbach on the Neckar River. Although he studied law and medicine, he preferred literature. He became a writer at the Mannheim Theater, a professor of history at Jena, and a friend of Goethe at Weimar.

Schiller wrote many plays dealing with classical ideals, especially freedom. His characters deal with human problems and must make important decisions. In *Maria Stuart* the Scottish Queen, Mary Stuart, accepts her unjust imprisonment by Elisabeth as atonement for her own misdeeds. In the patriotic play, *Wilhelm Tell*, the hero chooses between the possible death of his son and the freedom of the Swiss people. In the poem *An die Freude* ("Ode to Joy"), Schiller shares his belief that love can make the world a better place. Beethoven incorporated this poem into his *Ninth Symphony*.

Ernst Theodor Amadeus Hoffmann (1776–1822) was born in Königsberg on the Baltic Sea. Out of love for Mozart he changed his second middle name from Wilhelm to Amadeus. He was also an ardent fan of Beethoven. Too much work and lack of enough attention to his health led to his early death.

E.T.A. Hoffmann's writing has influenced authors in other nations, especially Charles Baudelaire in France and Edgar Allan Poe in the United States. A collection of his stories called *Nachtstücke* inspired Offenbach's opera, *Les Contes d'Hoffmann*. *Nußknacker und Mäusekönig* inspired Tchaikowsky's musical work, *The Nutcracker Suite*. The stories of Hoffmann are Romantic. They deal with imagination, and the many opposites in everyday life; joy and sorrow, good and evil, and dreams and reality.

 Ende gut, alles gut.   All's well, that ends well.

The poet, playwright, and essayist Else Lasker-Schüler (1869-1945) was born in Elberfeld, a small village near Wuppertal. She was raised in a warm and loving home and was devastated when her parents and brother died. Eventually she found some consolation in literature and art. Historical practices and traditions had made it difficult for most women to be well educated, but changes in the late nineteenth and early twentieth centuries provided increased opportunities for women authors. Lasker-Schüler took advantage of the opportunities and joined the exciting circle of Berlin's Expressionists. She contributed to new literary magazines and wrote several volumes of poetry and prose that she decorated with her own lithographs and drawings. Her works were praised by such distinguished celebrities as poet Gottfried Benn and Franz Marc, an artist in the famous "Blue Rider" community.

Later years brought the poet a renewed sense of loss, as her second marriage failed and her son died. When the literary and political climate of Berlin changed, Lasker-Schüler emigrated to Palestine and lived in Jerusalem until her death.

Most of Lasker-Schüler's poems, in volumes entitled *Styx, Der siebente Tag,* and *Hebräische Balladen,* focus on the themes of love, friendship, and loss. They show the poet's unusual use of language, contain colorful imagery and references to mythology, and, in general, reflect the free spirit of the Expressionist movement. Lasker-Schüler is a respected leader in early twentieth century literature. Gottfried Benn called her the greatest woman lyric poet of Germany.

Christa Wolf is a contemporary novelist and literary critic. She was born in 1929 in Landsberg, a small town once in Germany but now in Poland. Her parents owned a small store and Wolf enjoyed a quiet middle-class upbringing. World War II, however, and its aftermath brought harsh realities and severe hardships. Her family had to join the thousands of refugees who were forced to leave their homes and march westward.

After secondary school in 1949, Wolf began to identify with the political and social ideals of the new German Democratic Republic. University studies and discussions with the well-established author Anna Seghers helped the young woman decide on a literary career.

Wolf's first novel, *Der geteilte Himmel,* received tremendous worldwide attention and soon appeared as a motion picture. It concerns two young people whose lives and love are disrupted by the politics of East versus West. A second novel, *Nachdenken über Christa W.,* and other stories show how societies and governments can interfere with an individual's personal liberty and self-esteem.

Exercises

A Guess who...

1. loved the music of Mozart and Beethoven. _____

2. was a statesman and scientist as well as an author. _____

3. was an artist as well as a writer. _____

4. studied medicine. _____

5. wrote about politics and love. _____

B Verbinde B mit A.

A	B
1. Elsc Lasker-Schüler _____	a. Schiller
2. "Romantic" stories _____	b. are about ideals.
3. Friedrich _____	c. Expressionist poet
4. "Classical" stories _____	d. Hoffmann
5. Ernst Theodor Amadeus _____	e. are about dreams and imagination.

C Using the example, complete the chart below.

Name of work	Author	Type of Musical Rendition	Composer(s)
example			
Wilhelm Tell (William Tell)	Schiller	opera	Rossini
1. *Nachtstücke* (Night-Pieces)	_____	_____	_____
2. *An die Freude* (Ode to Joy)	_____	_____	_____
3. *Nußknacker und Mäusekönig* (Nutcracker and Mouse-King)	_____	_____	_____
4. *Faust*	_____	_____	_____
			_____

D Complete the analogies.

1. plays and poetry: Schiller = _____: Hoffmann

2. Goethe: _____ = Schiller: *Maria Stuart*

3. Königsberg: Hoffmann = _____: Schiller

4. _____: knowledge = *Wilhelm Tell*: freedom

5. "Ode to Joy": _____ = *Nutcracker and Mouse-King*: story

6. _____: C. Wolf = poems: Lasker-Schüler

E Which author would most likely...

1. encourage a child to get a well-rounded education? _____

2. enjoy creating new words and puns? _____

3. explain historical events in Europe? _____

4. write a script for a horror or science-fiction film? _____

5. help a child develop personal goals and self-esteem? _____

6. wear an "I Love Mozart and Beethoven" T-shirt? _____

F Label each plot described below as either Classical or Romantic.

1. Eunice Unity is working this summer at Camp Ideal. Her job is to organize the children into activity groups and to direct a variety show for the benefit of underprivileged children. On this particular day the campers are squabbling about who has the most talent and who will perform first. Eunice arrives on the scene, and in a short time transforms the children from selfish creatures into helpful and compassionate young people.

_____

2. While riding your horse one late moonlit evening, you come to a fork in the road. A sign pointing to the left says: "This way to that way." A sign pointing to the right says: "That way to this way." Just as you are about to make your decision, a cloud passes in front of the moon, an owl shrieks and a bat flies into your face.

_____

G Verbinde den Namen mit der Abbildung!

Hoffmann

Goethe

Schiller

Ergänze die Sätze!

1. _____ taught history at the university in Jena.

2. _____ had a great influence on literature in France and the United States.

3. _____ was a friend of Anna Seghers.

4. _____ was exceptionally good in everything he studied.

5. _____ was interested in the choices and decisions people had to make.

6. _____ wrote unusual lyric poetry.

7. _____ was put into jail by Queen Elisabeth.

8. _____ was a national hero in Switzerland.

9. _____ und _____ inspired Tchaikowsky.

10. _____ made a deal with the devil in exchange for knowledge.

DEUTSCHES THEATER

19.30 Uhr
Premiere

August Strindberg

DIE GESPENSTERSONATE

Solter Nikulka Stromberg Bredemeyer Bolle Geisler Hayner Hischer Klein I. Schweighöfer Wachowiak Bergermann Grashof Huth Mellies Schulze Solter Stempel

---

19.30 Uhr

August Strindberg

DIE GESPENSTERSONATE

siehe 1. Oktober

11.00 Uhr
D-Matinee

Volker Braun

DER WENDEHALS

oder Trotzdestonichts oder Wenigerdestonichts

Es lesen:
Volker Braun, Jörg Gudzuhn und Thomas Langhoff

19.30–22.15 Uhr

Carlo Goldoni

DER DIENER ZWEIER HERREN

Rudolph Loepelmann Fischer Hayner Weißenborn v. Zglinicki Baur Falkenau Hiemer Just Latchinian Mann Morgenroth Walke Ziethen

---

19.00–22.15 Uhr

Hugo von Hofmannsthal

DER TURM

Langhoff Hein Harnisch Hilprecht Wachowiak Weißenborn v. Zglinicki Bading Baur Berlin Böwe Borgelt Esche Gudzuhn Hiemer Huth Kirchner Körner Kradolfer Kranzkowski Lienert Mann Marggraf Mellies Möck Morgenroth Piontek Schneider Schulze Schweighöfer Trommer Walke
(Koproduktion mit den Wiener Festwochen)

20.00–22.15 Uhr

EBERHARD ESCHE spricht

REINEKE FUCHS

von Johann Wolfgang v. Goethe

19.00–22.30 Uhr

Heinrich v. Kleist

DAS KÄTHCHEN VON HEILBRONN

Langhoff Hein Neumann Hilprecht Heinz Hischer Klein Krumbiegel Manzel Perdelwitz Reichel Tempelhof Baur Böwe Borgelt Dimke Förster Gudzuhn Hiemer Körner Kradolfer Kranzkowski Manz Morgenroth Neumann Piontek Schulze Weinheimer Ziethen

---

19.30–22.30 Uhr

Friedrich Schiller

MARIA STUART

Langhoff Troike Schreiber Hilprecht Grube-Deister Ritter Wachowiak Bergermann Böwe Falkenau Gudzuhn Lienert Pietzsch Piontek Schneider Trettau

---

19.00–23.15 Uhr

Henrik Ibsen

PEER GYNT

Solter Nikulka Stromberg Schambach Morgenroth Geisler Hayner Hischer Schnitzler Schorn Staack Wachowiak Weißenborn Zion Bergermann Huth Köllner Lebinsky Manz Marggraf Mellies Möck Pietzsch Scholz Shabaviz Stempel Walke Ziethen

---

22.00 Uhr · D-Foyer

Wilhelm Reich

REDE AN DEN KLEINEN MANN mit IGNAZ KIRCHNER

21.00 Uhr
D-Baracke
Schumannstr. 10

Philip Ridley

DER DISNEY-KILLER

Latchinian Becker Klein Latchinian Walke Wandtke

16.00–23.00 Uhr

Heiner Müller

HAMLET/HAMLETMASCHINE

Müller Wonder Stromberg Bendokat Bolle Broich Manzel Taudte Gudzuhn Kind Kranzkowski Lienert Marggraf Mühe Möck Neumann Piontek Suschke Weinheimer Wuttke

---

KAMMERSPIELE

1 FREITAG

Bernard Shaw — 19.30–21.30 Uhr

LÄNDLICHE WERBUNG

Piontek Šramek v. Zglinicki Esche

---

2 SONNABEND

Franca Rame/Dario Fo — 19.30–21.30 Uhr

OFFENE ZWEIERBEZIEHUNG

siehe 25. Oktober

---

3 SONNTAG

Ausstellungseröffnung — 17.30 Uhr · Foyer
Dokumentarausstellung im Rahmen
„norsk kultur · Norwegen-Berlin '93"

IBSEN IN DEUTSCHLAND

Klaus Piontek liest aus Shaws IBSENBREVIER
Geöffnet bis 24.10.1993 zu den Vorstellungen

Henrik Ibsen — 19.30–22.30 Uhr

JOHN GABRIEL BORKMAN

Castorf Schubert Bendokat Bolle Klein I. Schweighöfer Lebinsky M. Schweighöfer Wandtke

Franca Rame/Dario Fo — 19.30–21.30 Uhr

OFFENE ZWEIERBEZIEHUNG

Medina Schubert Manzel Neumann

---

4 MONTAG

---

5 DIENSTAG

Gerhart Hauptmann — 19.30–22.15 Uhr

DER BIBERPELZ

siehe 24. Oktober

Bernard Shaw — 19.30–21.30 Uhr

LÄNDLICHE WERBUNG

Piontek Šramek v. Zglinicki Esche

---

6 MITTWOCH

---

7 DONNERSTAG

Carl Sternheim — 19.30–21.15 Uhr
keine Pause

DER NEBBICH

Rudolph Hegi Gawlich Manzel Baur Hiemer Hilprecht Kleinert Kranzkowski Mann Schweighöfer Stempel Walke Wandtke Weinheimer

Lothar Trolle — 20.00–21.30 Uhr

MANEGE FREI FÜR EINE ÄLTERE DAME oder WSTAWATE, LIZZY, WSTAWATE

Rese Keienburg Hilprecht
Es spielt GUDRUN RITTER

---

8 FREITAG

Henrik Ibsen — 19.30–22.15 Uhr

GESPENSTER

Langhoff Hein Hilprecht Keller v. Zglinicki Böwe Körner Mühe

---

9 SONNABEND

---

10 SONNTAG

Irene Dische — 11.00 Uhr
D-Lesung bei laufendem Einlaß und offenem Ende

EIN FREMDES GEFÜHL oder VERÄNDERUNGEN ÜBER EINEN DEUTSCHEN

Die Autorin und 33 Schauspieler des Deutschen Theaters präsentieren die 33 Kapitel des neuen Romans

---

Der grosse Märchenschatz

BREITSCHOPF

Berger
Der große Märchenschatz
Entzückend illustrierte, liebe
alte Märchen, neu erzählt. Für
Legastheniker geeignet.
192 S., Großformat

J + M ab 7

MEIN BUNTES MÄRCHENBUCH

SAMMELBAND

Fräulein Wildfang

Deutsche Oper Berlin
Berlin-Charlottenburg, Bismarckstraße

Hochparkett
Loge-Mitte
RECHTS

Sitz Nr.
2

NACH DER VORSTELLUNG
IN
„Die Theater-Klauße"
Knesebeckstraße 4
Gegenüber dem Renaissance-Theater

... me Küche täglich außer Sa bis 24 Uhr

Theater	Mo., 3. Okt.	Di., 4. Okt.	Mi., 5. Okt.	Do., 6. Okt.	Fr., 7. Okt.	Sa., 8. Okt.	So., 9. Okt.
Altonaer Th. Museumstr. 17 **Vorverkauf Chemnitzstr. 82 Tel. 39 15 45/46**	20–22 Uhr	20–22 Uhr	16.30–18.30 U. 20–22 Uhr	20–22 Uhr	20–22 Uhr	16.30–18.30 U. 20–22 Uhr	19–21 Uhr

Maria Stuart Trauerspiel v. **Friedrich Schiller**
Regie: Hans Fitze, Bühnenbild u. Kostüme: Susanne Weil-v. Steimker
mit Karen Hüttmann, Veronika Kranich, Peter v. Schultz, Manfred Wohlers, Werner Hoffmann, Frank Straass, Thomas Karallus, Hanni Hagel, Lothar Zibell, Günter Beurenmeister, Claus Wagner, Albert Lichtenfeld u. v. a.

18 LEISURE AND RECREATION
Freizeit

Wohin gehst du? Where are you going?

Ich gehe zum Fußballspiel.
I'm going to the soccer game.

Ich gehe ins Museum.
I'm going to the museum.

Ich gehe auf die Party.
I'm going to the party.

Ich gehe zum Strand.
I'm going to the beach.

Andreas:	Wohin gehst du heute abend?	Where are you going tonight?
Heiko:	Ich gehe zum Fußballspiel.	I'm going to the soccer game.
Andreas:	Ich auch.	Me, too.

❁ ❁ ❁ ❁ ❁

Peter:	Was machst du heute?	What are you doing today?
Tina:	Ich gehe ins Museum...in die Alte Pinakothek*.	I'm going to the museum...to the *Alte Pinakothek.*
Peter:	Was ist da los?	What's going on there?
Tina:	Das Dürerfest findet diese Woche statt.	The Dürer Festival is taking place this week.

* The Alte Pinakothek, *an art museum in München, houses paintings and artworks from the 14th to the 18th centuries. Its counterpart, the* Neue Pinakothek, *contains art generally from the 19th and 20th centuries.*

 In der Abwechslung liegt das Vergnügen. Variety is the spice of life.

Ich spiele Volleyball.
I play volleyball.

Ich spiele Fußball.
I play soccer.

Welche Sportart treibst du?
What sports do you play?

Ich spiele Basketball.
I play basketball.

Ich spiele Tennis.
I play tennis.

Ich spiele Baseball.
I play baseball.

Käthe:	Morgen machen wir ein Picknick.	Tomorrow we'll have a picnic.
Julia:	Wo denn?	Where's that?
Käthe:	Am Strand. Willst du mitkommen?	At the beach. Do you want to come along?
Julia:	Ja. Ich schwimme gern.	Yes. I like swimming.

❀❀❀❀❀

Jutta:	Gehst du heute abend auf die Party?	Are you going to the party tonight?
Thomas:	Na klar. Gibt es da Musik?	Of course. Will there be music?
Jutta:	Ja. Ich tanze gern.	Yes. I like dancing.

A Wohin gehst du? Ergänze die Sätze auf deutsch!

1. Ich gehe zu einem _____ . (*soccer game*)

2. Ich gehe zu einem _____ . (*picnic*)

3. Ich gehe auf eine _____ . (*party*)

4. Ich gehe in ein _____ . (*museum*)

5. Ich gehe zum _____ . (*beach*)

B Select the correct answers based on the previous dialogues.

1. Wann ist das Fußballspiel?
   a. am Montag
   b. um vier Uhr
   c. heute abend
   d. in zwei Wochen

2. Was ist die Alte Pinakothek?
   a. ein Strand
   b. ein Rad
   c. ein Dürerfest
   d. ein Museum

3. Wer ist Dürer?
   a. ein Lehrer
   b. ein Onkel
   c. ein Museum
   d. ein Künstler

4. Wann ist das Picknick?
   a. morgen
   b. heute
   c. am Sonntag
   d. um ein Uhr

5. Wo ist das Picknick?
   a. am Mittwoch
   b. am Dienstag
   c. am Strand
   d. am Museum

C Welche Sportart treibst du? Ergänze die Sätze auf deutsch!

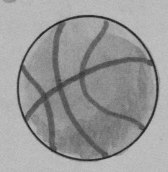

1. Ich spiele _____ .

2. Ich spiele _____ .

3. Ich spiele _____ .

4. Ich spiele _____ .

5. Ich spiele _____ .

D Schreib die Wörter richtig.

1. FRTZEEII _____

2. NSDATR _____

3. KSUIM _____

4. WIMMSCHEN _____

5. REENTI _____

E Was machst du gern? Ergänze die Sätze auf deutsch!

1. Ich _____ gern Ski.

2. Ich _____ gern.

3. Ich _____ gern ein
   Buch.

4. Ich _____ gern Rad.

5. Ich _____ gern.

6. Ich _____ gern.

F   Ergänze den Dialog auf deutsch.

Timo: Was machst _____ am Freitag abend?

Ali: _____ gehe zu Christines Haus.

Timo: Was ist da _____ ?

Ali: Eine Party _____ da statt.

Timo: Wie viele kommen zur _____ ?

Ali: Neun. Fünf _____ und vier Jungen.

Timo: Gut. Ich _____ auch. Gibt es da auch

_____ ?

Ali: Na klar. Ich tanze _____ .

G   Lies den Absatz! Wähle die richtigen Antworten!

Martina plant eine Geburtstagsparty am Strand. Heute ist sie zwölf Jahre alt. Am Samstag wird sie dreizehn. Wer kommt zur Party? Ihre Freunde: Anja, Luise, Patrick, Boris und Dieter. Die Party ist um drei Uhr. Ihre Freunde sind froh. Sie spielen gern Volleyball. Sie schwimmen, tanzen und machen auch ein Picknick. Eine Geburtstagsparty am Strand ist eine prima Idee!

die Geburtstagsparty	birthday party
wird	(she will) turn, become
Freunde	friends
froh	happy
prima	terrific

1. Wie alt ist Martina heute?
    a. dreizehn   c. drei
    b. zwölf   d. elf

2. Wie viele Jungen kommen zur Party?
    a. drei   c. dreizehn
    b. zwölf   d. zwei

3. Wann ist Martinas Geburtstag?
    a. am Sonntag   c. am Donnerstag
    b. am Montag   d. am Samstag

4. Wo essen die Mädchen und Jungen gern?
    a. in einem Restaurant   c. in der Küche
    b. am Strand   d. im Eßzimmer

5. Was machen die Jungen und Mädchen gern?
    a. Sie schreiben gern.   c. Sie wiederholen gern.
    b. Sie schwimmen gern.   d. Sie lesen gern.

ARD

SA 25.9.
9.03 Ping Pong
9.45–13.00 ARD/ZDF-Vormittagsprogramm
13.05 Europamagazin
13.30 Nachbarn
14.15 Songs im Saloon
14.45 Das Beste aus „Freut Euch des Nordens"
15.30 Weltreisen
16.05 Disney Club
17.30 Sportschau
18.10 Kinderquatsch mit Michael Talkshow
18.40 Rudis Tiershow
19.50 Lottozahlen
20.00 Tagesschau
20.15 Starflight One – Irrflug ins All US-Katastrophenfilm (1982) im Raumfahrt-Milieu
22.05 Tagesthemen
22.30 Brennende Herzen Live-Unterhaltung
23.15 James Bond: Der Mann mit dem goldenen Colt
1.15 Solo für O.N.C.E.L. Der Mann im grünen Hut

SO 26.9.
7.30 Disney Club
8.55 Berlin-Marathon
11.30 Die Maus
12.00 Presseclub
13.15 Neues vom Süderhof
13.45 Degrassi High
14.10 A–Z Lifeshow
14.30 Vier unter einem Dach
15.05 Sport extra
17.00 Ratgeber: Geld
17.30 Gott und die Welt
18.10 Sportschau
18.40 Lindenstraße
19.10 Weltspiegel
20.00 Tagesschau
20.15 Tatort Um Haus und Hof. Krimireihe mit Manfred Krug
21.50 Kulturweltspiegel
22.20 Tagesthemen
22.35 Sowieso
23.05 Zwei Frauen Dt. Spielfilm (1988/89)
0.50 Und morgen werd' ich weinen US-Spielfilm (1955) mit Susan Hayward

MO 27.9.
6.00–13.00 ARD/ZDF-Vormittagsprogramm
13.45 Wirtschaftstelegramm
14.02 Die Maus
14.30 Sechs Richtige
15.03 Ich und meine Schwiegersöhne
16.30 Fussbroichs (4)
17.05 Punkt 5/Länderreport
17.15 Pssst . . . Ratespiel
17.55 Forstinspektor Buchholz Blindgänger
18.55 Zwei Halbe sind noch
20.00 Tagesschau
20.15 Herzblatt Eine Show zum Verlieben mit Rainhard Fendrich
21.00 FAKT Magazin
21.40 Detektivbüro Roth Fallrückzieher. Krimiserie
22.30 Tagesthemen
23.00 Tatort Krimireihe
0.35 Ernst sein ist alles Engl. Spielfilm (1952) mit Michael Redgrave

DI 28.9.
6.00–13.00 ARD/ZDF-Vormittagsprogramm
13.45 Wirtschaftstelegramm
14.02 Floris Zapp Zarapp
14.30 Sechs Richtige
15.03 Die Trickfilmschau
15.15 Fußball-Europacup Wladikawkas – Dortmund UEFA-Pokal, 1. Rd. Rückspiel
17.30 Punkt 5/Länderreport
17.55 Feuer und Flamme
18.25 Marienhof
18.55 Großstadtrevier
20.00 Tagesschau
20.15 Peter Strohm Tote zahlen nicht. Krimiserie mit Klaus Löwitsch
21.05 Wiedersehen mit Loriot (4)
21.30 Plusminus
22.05 Golden Girls
22.30 Tagesthemen
23.00 Boulevard Bio
0.00 Magnum Krimireihe
0.50 Ehe im Schatten Dt. Spielfilm (1947)

MI 29.9.
6.00–13.00 ARD/ZDF-Vormittagsprogramm
13.45 Wirtschaftstelegramm
14.02 Sesamstraße
14.30 Sechs Richtige
15.03 Ping Pong
15.30 Talk täglich
16.03 Frauengeschichten
16.30 Fussbroichs (5)
17.05 Punkt 5/Länderreport
17.15 Pssst . . . Ratespiel
17.55 Die glückliche Familie
18.55 Wildbach TV-Serie
20.00 Tagesschau
20.15 Keine Angst vor Zoff Heide Simonis – die Neue in Kiel. Erste Frau an der Spitze eines Bundeslandes
20.50 Politogramm: Skala
21.00 Die Männer vom K 3
22.30 Tagesthemen
23.05 Faruch, mein Bruder Tadschikischer Spielfilm ('91)
0.45 Der Mann für Mord US-Kriminalfilm (1935) mit Spencer Tracy

DO 30.9.
6.00–13.00 ARD/ZDF-Vormittagsprogramm
13.45 Wirtschaftstelegramm
14.02 Kinderprogramm
15.30 Talk täglich
16.03 Bericht: Sabine Christiansen
16.30 Durchgehend warme Küche (14) Der Fall O.
17.05 Punkt 5/Länderreport
17.15 Pssst . . .
17.55 Feuer und Flamme
18.25 Marienhof
18.55 Der Fahnder
20.00 Tagesschau
20.15 Saat der Gewalt Reportage
21.03 Geschichten aus der Heimat Hase und Igel, Serie mit Harald Juhnke
22.00 Menschen mit Herz
22.30 Tagesthemen
23.00 Bücherjournal
0.00 Vier x Herman
0.30 Mitternacht Canale Grande US-Spielfilm ('66)

FR 1.10.
6.00–13.00 ARD/ZDF-Vormittagsprogramm
13.45 Wirtschaftstelegramm
14.02 Sesamstraße
14.30 Wunder der Erde
15.20 Wo die Lilien blühen
17.05 Punkt 5/Länderreport
17.15 Pssst . . . Ratespiel
17.55 Auf Achse
18.55 Mr. Bean spezial
19.25 Herzblatt Show mit Reinhard Fendrich
20.00 Tagesschau
20.15 Magnum Der heiße Schnee auf Hawaii. Pilotfilm zur Krimiserie mit Tom Selleck u. a.
21.40 ARD – exklusiv
22.30 Tagesthemen
23.00 Sportschau
23.25 Nachtschwester Kroymann Neue Satireshow
23.55 F.I.S.T – Ein Mann geht seinen Weg US-Spielfilm mit Sylvester Stallone
2.05 Miami Vice

Besucht die

Sesselbahn

in Cochem
— ein lohnendes Ausflugsziel —

Ausgangspunkt vieler Wanderwege

Herrlicher Panoramablick

Freizeitangebote

Terrassen-Café-Restaurant

Großer Parkplatz

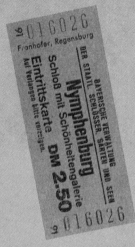

DA MACHT EUROPA SPASS

EUROPA★PARK

D-7631 Rust · Tel. 07822/77-0 · A5 Karlsruhe-Basel Ausfahrt Ettenheim oder Herbolzheim
Berechtigt zum kostenlosen Parken

HISTORISCHER SCHÄFERTANZ
ROTHENBURG OB DER TAUBER

Marktplatz Stehplatz: DM 1,50
einschließlich Notgroschen DM —,10
zugunsten der Stadt Rothenburg ob der Tauber

Die Karte ist sichtbar zu tragen

Freikarte
(bei der städt. Steuerstelle angemeldet)

Bei Unterbrechung oder Ausfall des Tanzes infolge höherer Gewalt (Unwetter, Regen usw.) besteht kein Anspruch auf Rückerstattung des Eintrittspreises

SHOPPING
Einkaufen

der Verkäufer
salesclerk

die Kundin
customer

die Tennisschuhe
tennis shoes

Ich kaufe im Einkaufszentrum ein.
I shop at the shopping center (mall).

Anne:	Wohin gehst du?	Where are you going?
Kurt:	Zum Einkaufszentrum.	To the shopping center.
Anne:	Was kaufst du dort?	What are you going to buy there?
Kurt:	Tennisschuhe.	Tennis shoes.

✾✾✾✾✾

Verkäufer:	Guten Morgen! Was darf es sein?	Good morning! May I help you?
Kundin:	Ich möchte ein Buch kaufen.	I would like to buy a book.
Verkäufer:	Gut. Unsere Auswahl ist sehr groß.	Good. Our selection is very large.

 Wer zuerst kommt, mahlt zuerst. First come, first served.

Kunde:	Wieviel kostet diese CD?	How much is this CD?
Kassiererin:	Sie kostet 32 Mark.	It costs 32 marks.
Kunde:	Das ist teuer!	That's expensive!
Kassiererin:	Nein, das ist billig.	No, that's cheap.
Kunde:	Gut. Ich kaufe die CD. Hier ist das Geld.	OK. I'll buy the CD. Here is the money.
Kassiererin:	Danke schön. Da ist Ihr Kleingeld.	Thank you very much. There's your change.

| Verkäuferin: | Noch etwas? | Anything else? |
| Kunde: | Hm...drei Tomaten, fünf Pfirsiche und grüne Bohnen. Ja, das ist alles. | Uhm...three tomatoes, five peaches and green beans. Yes, that's all. |

A Match the name of the place in column B with what you can buy there in column A.

<table>
<tr><td>A</td><td></td><td>B</td></tr>
<tr><td>1. Tennisschuhe</td><td>_____</td><td>a. market</td></tr>
<tr><td>2. grüne Bohnen</td><td>_____</td><td>b. shoe store</td></tr>
<tr><td>3. CD</td><td>_____</td><td>c. furniture store</td></tr>
<tr><td>4. Stuhl</td><td>_____</td><td>d. stationery store</td></tr>
<tr><td>5. Kulis und Hefte</td><td>_____</td><td>e. music store</td></tr>
</table>

B Ergänze jeden Satz mit dem Wort für das Bild!

1. Ich möchte _____

   kaufen.

2. Frau Lopez kauft viel Obst auf dem

   _____ .

3. Ich gehe zum

   _____ .

4. Hier ist Ihr _____ ,

   Herr Hoffmann.

5. Die CD ist billig. Sie kostet 23

   _____ .

C Choose the word from the following list that completes each sentence correctly.

Kleingeld   Eis   Geld   kaufen

teuer   geht   kosten

Timo möchte eine CD _____ . Er

_____ zum Einkaufszentrum. Die CDs

_____ heute nur sechzehn Mark. Das ist nicht

_____ . Timo hat zwanzig Mark. Die Verkäuferin gibt

Timo vier Mark _____ . Er geht dann in ein Café und

kauft dort für vier Mark ein _____ . Jetzt hat Timo

kein _____ mehr.

D Wähle die richtige Antwort!

1. If you see the sign "reduzierter Preis," how would you expect the price of the
   object to be?
   a. billig   c. schön
   b. teuer   d. grün

2. What do you reply if the cashier says "Das macht 110 Mark"?
   a. Wo ist das Geschäft?   c. Hier ist das Geld.
   b. Ich kaufe auf dem Markt ein.   d. Was kaufst du dort?

3. What do you get back if you give the cashier too much money?
   a. Auswahl   c. Markt
   b. Kasse   d. Kleingeld

4. Who helps you find what you need?
   a. der Verkäufer oder die   c. der Kassierer oder die Kassiererin
      Verkäuferin
   b. der Kunde oder die Kundin   d. der Landwirt oder die Landwirtin

5. What do you say if you want to find out about the price?
   a. Wieviel Uhr ist es?   c. Wieviel Geld haben Sie?
   b. Wieviel kostet es?   d. Wieviel ist neun und zwölf?

E Welche Antwort ist richtig?

1. Noch etwas?
   a. Ja. Ich spiele Fußball.
   b. Ja. Ein Buch, bitte.
   c. Nein. Ich habe Geld.
   d. Nein. Ich kaufe im Geschäft ein.

2. Warum gehst du auf den Markt?
   a. Ich möchte Bananen und Birnen kaufen.
   b. Dort gibt es keine Auswahl.
   c. Es ist da sehr teuer.
   d. Ich komme mit.

3. Ist die CD teuer?
   a. Ja. Es ist eine CD.
   b. Nein. Sie ist billig.
   c. Nein. Sie ist schön.
   d. Ja. Sie ist groß.

4. Wieviel kosten die Tennisschuhe?
   a. Eine Auswahl.
   b. Ein reduzierter Preis.
   c. Viele Pfirsiche.
   d. Viel Geld.

5. Was darf es sein?
   a. Ich habe kein Kleingeld.
   b. Nein, das ist nicht billig.
   c. Ich möchte ein Heft kaufen.
   d. Das kostet viel Geld.

F You are in a clothing store. Complete the conversation between you, the customer, and the salesclerk.

Verkäufer: Guten Tag.

Du: Guten _____ .

Verkäufer: Was darf es _____ , bitte?

Du: Ich _____ ein Hemd kaufen.

Verkäufer: Hier _____ unsere Auswahl. Sie ist sehr groß.

Du: Dieses Hemd hier hat eine schöne _____ .

Verkäufer: Ja, blau ist sehr schön.

Du: Wieviel kostet das _____ ?

Verkäufer: Nur 38 _____ . Heute ist es ein

reduzierter _____ .

Du: Gut. Ich _____ es.

Verkäufer: Prima. Die _____ ist dort.

Kreuzworträtsel

G

Vertical	Horizontal

Vertical

1. "Herr Pigini wohnt in Berlin. ...kommt aus Italien."
2. "Das Haus kostet viel...."
3. "reduzierter..."
4. "Frau Lehmann hat viele Kleider. ...hat eine große Auswahl."
5. a popular place for buying fruits and vegetables
6. "Wieviel...diese CD?"
7. "Die Auswahl im Einkaufszentrum ist sehr...." (ß = SS)
8. "Wo ist...Kasse?"
12. "Ich...im Geschäft ein."
13. "Willi kauft Bananen, Birnen und grüne...."
17. "In diesem Geschäft gibt es eine große...."
18. "...gehst du jetzt? Auf den Markt."
19. "Ist der Computer billig? Nein, er ist...."
20. "...kaufe heute ein."

Horizontal

3. "Obst"
6. one or more coins
9. the opposite of "hier"
10. "...kostet 90 Mark."
11. "Renate hat...schönes Kleid."
12. it contains coins and bills
14. "Herr Kinski ist...Kassierer in diesem Geschäft."
15. "...ist der Markt?"
16. "...Einkaufszentrum ist in der Stadt."
19. what you need to play a certain kind of sport
21. the person waited on by a salesclerk
22. "Maria und Natascha gehen um acht Uhr...die Klasse."
23. the opposite of "dort" or "da"
24. "Ist das Hemd teuer? Nein, es ist...."

Knackig & frisch!

Span. Tomaten Kl.I 1 kg **1.99**

Ital. Trauben Kl. I „Italia" 1,5-kg-Schale **2.99**

BASKETBALL
PREIS-TIP
Größe 36 BIS 46
9
ab **29.95**

PREIS
Damen-Hausschuhe
19.90

17 SOLO Mofa „Super Luxus 25" mit Flüssigkeitskühlung und hydraulischer Kupplung Hydrodrive, in 1- oder 2-Gang-Vollautomatik. Motor SOLO. Aluminium-Druckgußfelgen, Teleskop-Vordergabel, Teleskop-Hinterrad-Federbeine, Edelstahl-Schutzbleche, 5-Liter-Tourentank, breiter Schwingsattel, Lenkerschloß.

1-Gang rot 005.312 DM **1279.-**
2-Gang rot 005.313 DM **1429.-**
SOLO Moped „Super Luxus 50" wie vor, jedoch 1,77 kW (= 2,4 PS) und 50 km/h, zusätzlich mit Tachometer und Rückspiegel.
2-Gang rot 007.805 DM **1499.-**

17
SOLO-Mofas, bewährte deutsche Marken-Fabrikation
ab **1279.-**

Technische Daten:
SOLO-Mofa-Moped – Tankinhalt: 5 Liter, Zweitakt-Mischung mit Normal-Benzin bleifrei. Federung: Teleskop-Gabel vorn. Hinterrad-Federbeine. Leistung: Mofa 1,18 kW (= 1,6 PS); Moped 1,77 kW (= 2,4 PS). Motor: SOLO 1-Zylinder-2-Takt-Motor, 1 bzw. 2-Gang.

975

*Liebevolle Landmoden
Karin Hummel
- Galerie Freßgass -
Große Bockenheimer Straße 52
6000 Frankfurt / Main 1
Telefon 0 69 / 29 26 26*

30 WATT Maximale Leistung
● Super Bass System
● Full Logical-Laufwerke
● CD-Schublade
13 | **699.-**

UNIVERSUM

**Hier geht's rund!
Alle mit CD**

11 Bespielte Mini-Discs
George Michael „Faith"	339.951	
Michael	514.672	
Michael Bolton „Timeless (The Classics)"	185.462	
Mariah Carey „Emotions"	571.982	
Gloria Estafan & MSM „Greatest Hits"	186.361	
Bruce Springsteen „Human Touch"	187.260	
Paul Young „From Time to Time"	188.162	

je DM **36.95**

12 Unbespielte Mini-Discs
60 Minuten	254.123	5er-Pack	DM **109.75**
74 Minuten	199.922	5er-Pack	DM **124.75**

13 UNIVERSUM Stereo-Radio-Recorder mit Doppel-Cassettendeck und CD-Player. PLL-Tuner mit UKW-Stereo/MW/LW. 40 Stationsspeicher. Automatischer/manueller Suchlauf. Preset Scan. Full Logic-Laufwerke. Autoreverse. High Speed Dubbing. Continuous Play. CD-Synchro. Bandselector. CD-Player in Schubladentechnik. 10er-Musik-Kalender. Repeat, Intro-Scan, Zufallswiedergabe und CD Edit-Funktion. 16 Titel programmierbar. 2× 15 Watt Maximalleistung. Super Bass System und 4 vorprogrammierte Klangeinstellungen für Linear/Pop/Rock/Klassik. Infrarot-Fernbedienung für Rundfunk, Cassetten- und CD-Player-Betrieb sowie elektronische Lautstärkeregelung. Batterie- und Netzbetrieb. Maße ca.: B. 58, H. 22, T. 28 cm.
Bestell-Nr. 065.979 DM **699.-**

1285

Wie reist du?

How do you travel?

Ich fliege.
I travel by plane.

Ich fahre mit dem Bus.
I travel by bus.

Ich fahre mit dem Auto.
I travel by car.

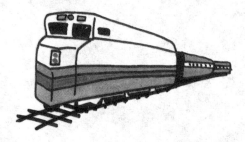

Ich fahre mit dem Zug.
I travel by train.

Ich fahre mit dem Schiff.
I travel by ship.

 Reisen bildet. Whoever travels far knows much.

die Angestellte
clerk

auf dem Flughafen
at the airport

der Reisepaß
passport

der Koffer
suitcase

der Schalter
ticket counter

der Reisende
traveler

Angestellte:	Ihren Reisepaß, bitte?	Your passport, please?
Reisender:	Er ist in meinem Koffer.	It's in my suitcase.
Angestellte:	Sie brauchen ihn, wenn Sie ankommen...bei der Paßkontrolle.	You'll need it when you arrive...at passport control.
Reisender:	Gut. Wo steht das Flugzeug?	OK. Where is the plane?
Angestellte:	Am Flugsteig 20. Dort drüben rechts. Gute Reise.	At gate 20. Over there, to the right. Have a nice trip.

Reisende:	Um wieviel Uhr fährt der nächste Zug nach Berlin?	What time does the next train for Berlin leave?
Angestellter:	Um zwölf Uhr. Hier ist der Fahrplan.	At twelve o'clock. Here's the schedule.
Reisende:	Danke. Ich möchte eine Rückfahrkarte, zweite Klasse.	I'd like a round-trip ticket, second class.
Angestellter:	Hier ist Ihre Fahrkarte. Das macht 200 Mark.	Here's your ticket. It's 200 marks.

| Herr Bodo: | Entschuldigen Sie. Wie komme ich zum Hotel Krone? | Excuse me. How do I get to Hotel Krone? |
| Frau Meier: | Fahren Sie mit dem Bus Nummer 2 und steigen Sie am Park aus. Das Hotel ist links. | Take bus number 2 and get off at the park. The hotel is on the left. |

Exercises

A Verbinde B mit A.

A

1. Gute Reise. _____
2. Entschuldigen Sie. _____
3. Sie brauchen einen Reisepaß. _____
4. Zweite Klasse, bitte. _____
5. Dort drüben, rechts. _____
6. Steigen Sie am Park aus. _____
7. Ich möchte eine Rückfahrkarte. _____
8. Es ist links. _____
9. Hier ist ein Fahrplan. _____
10. Das Flugzeug steht am Flugsteig. _____

B

a. Excuse me.

b. Over there, to the right.

c. The plane is at the gate.

d. Here's a schedule.

e. Get off at the park.

f. You need a passport.

g. Second class, please.

h. Have a nice trip.

i. I'd like a round-trip ticket.

j. It's on the left.

B Wie reist du? Ergänze die Sätze auf deutsch!

1. Ich _____ .

2. Ich _____ .

3. Ich _____ .

4. Ich _____ .

5. Ich _____ .

C Wähle die richtige Antwort.

1. Where do you find a train?
   - a. auf dem Flughafen
   - b. auf dem Bahnhof
   - c. bei der Paßkontrolle
   - d. auf der Straße

2. What do you ask if you want to buy a round-trip ticket?
   - a. Ich möchte eine Fahrkarte.
   - b. Ich möchte einen Reisepaß.
   - c. Ich möchte eine Paßkontrolle.
   - d. Ich möchte eine Rückfahrkarte.

3. What would you look at to find the times when trains, buses, planes, etc. arrive and leave?
   - a. der Fahrplan
   - b. der Bahnhof
   - c. der Flughafen
   - d. der Koffer

4. Where do you go at the airport to ask for information and to check your luggage?
   - a. das Flugzeug
   - b. die Straße
   - c. der Schalter
   - d. die Paßkontrolle

5. If you don't want a first-class ticket, what do you say?
   - a. Hier ist der Fahrplan.
   - b. Bus Nummer 2.
   - c. Dort drüben, rechts.
   - d. Zweite Klasse.

D Schreib die Wörter richtig.

1. GIUFLESTG _____

2. FEFKOR _____

3. PFNARAHL _____

4. CTRLSAHE _____

5. HFBAOHN _____

E Lies den Absatz und beantworte dann die Fragen.

Das Wetter ist heute warm und sonnig. Monika und Holger sind am Schalter im Hamburger Bahnhof. Sie sind froh. Sie machen heute eine Reise nach Köln. Holger bleibt bei den Koffern und Monika kauft zwei Fahrkarten. Dann gehen sie zum Bahnsteig, wo der Zug steht. Die Freunde steigen ein. Im Zug sitzt Monika am Fenster. Holger findet einen Platz am Gang. Auf der Reise sprechen sie von ihrem Besuch in Köln. Dort besuchen sie ihre Freunde. Monikas Onkel und Tante wohnen in Bonn, nicht weit von Köln entfernt. In Köln gibt es viel zu sehen und zu tun. Sie fahren fünf Stunden und kommen um vier Uhr im Kölner Bahnhof an. Dann steigen sie aus.

eine Reise machen	to take a trip
bleiben	to stay
der Bahnsteig	platform
der Platz am Gang	seat on the aisle
der Besuch	visit
nicht weit entfernt	not far away

1. Wie ist das Wetter?
   - a. schön
   - b. schlecht
   - c. nicht gut
   - d. kalt

2. Wo sind Monika und Holger?
   - a. auf dem Flughafen
   - b. auf dem Bahnhof
   - c. im Auto
   - d. im Flugzeug

3. Wie viele Fahrkarten kauft Monika?
   - a. eine
   - b. zwei
   - c. drei
   - d. vier

4. Wo steht der Zug?
   - a. am Fenster
   - c. am Schalter
   - c. am Bahnsteig
   - d. am Gang

5. Wo steigen Monika und Holger aus?
   - a. in Hamburg
   - b. in Köln
   - c. in Bonn
   - d. in Zürich

F Complete the analogies.

1. kaufen: Kunde = _____ : Reisender

2. Bahnhof: _____ = Flughafen: Flugzeug

3. Schiff: Ozean = Bus: _____

4. Flugsteig: Flughafen = _____ : Bahnhof

Kreuzworträtsel

Vertical   Horizontal

G

Vertical

1. Sie brauchen Ihren Reisepaß bei der....(ß = SS)
2. Um wieviel Uhr fährt der nächste...nach Hamburg?
3. "Zehn" auf englisch.
4. Sie brauchen den Reisepaß, wenn Sie...kommen.
5. ...wieviel Uhr beginnt das Konzert?
7. Die...steht am Schalter.
10. Ich finde einen Platz am....
11. Das Flugzeug steht am...20.
12. "Gehen" auf englisch.
13. "Nein" auf englisch.
18. Der Zug steht schon auf dem....
21. Holger und Monika sind.... Sie machen heute eine Reise.
24. "Sohn" auf englisch.

Horizontal

1. Holger findet einen...am Gang.
6. Die Freunde steigen in den Bus....
7. Der Zug steht...Bahnsteig.
8. ...Sie am Park aus.
9. Der Reisepaß ist...meinem Koffer.
11. Dort stehen viele Flugzeuge.
14. "Gut" auf englisch.
15. Heute ist es...heiß.
16. Monika...Holger fahren nach Köln.
17. Wie geht es Ihnen, Herr Böhme? ..., danke.
19. Dieter wohnt in Hamburg. ...ist 16 Jahre alt.
20. Wenn du nach Deutschland fliegst, dann brauchst du einen....
22. Der Teller, die Tasse und das Glas stehen auf dem....
23. ...ist heute warm und sonnig.
25. Wohin fliegt Herr Lehmann? ...fliegt nach München.
26. Die Freunde möchten im Sommer nach Österreich....

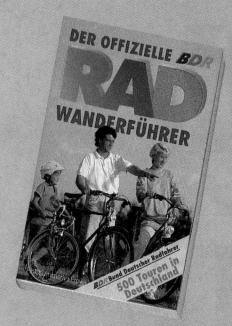

DER OFFIZIELLE *BDR*
RAD
WANDERFÜHRER

BDR Bund Deutscher Radfahrer
500 Touren in Deutschland

BRENNER
AUTOBAHN AG
Rennweg 19A
6020 Innsbruck

EINZELKARTE

Gem. § 52 der StVO sind Sie verpflichtet, an jeder Mautstelle anzuhalten und die Karte zur Entwertung vorzuweisen. Mautinkasso erfolgt für die Republik Österreich gemäß BGBL. 135/1964 i. d. g. F.

8.004/91-1

AUFZAHLUNG IN OES	INKASSO IN	PREIS IN OES INKL. 20% MWST.
		OES 130,00

041091 005   75 1138 BAAG 9

GÜLTIG BIS: 05.10   KAT A

I P E S H M B
N ☐ ☐ ☐ ☐ ☒ ☒ ☒ N
S ☐ ☐ ☐ ☐ ☐ ☐ ☐ S
22

„Historischer Schwarzwald-Expreß"
InterCity VT 601
Zielbahnhof: Donaueschingen

STADTWERKE FRANKFURT AM MAIN

00102101 284   16 10 -- 02.40

Standort   Tag   Uhrzeit   Preis

Nicht übertragbar. Es gelten die Gemeinsamen Beförderungsbedingungen und Tarifbestimmungen. Fahrscheine sind nach Beendigung der Fahrt bis nach Verlassen des Haltestellenbereichs aufzubewahren.

Der schnelle Weg nach Schweden.

SASSNITZ 4h TRELLEBORG

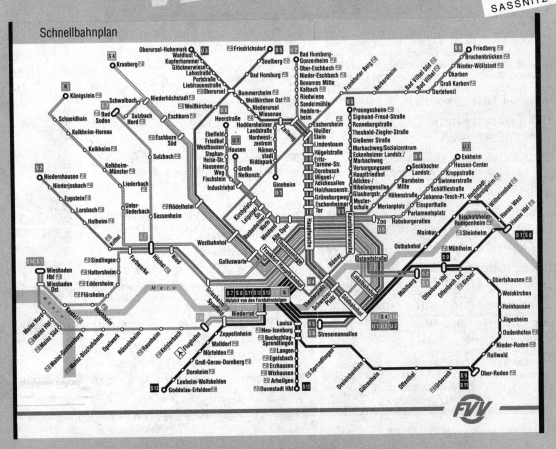

Schnellbahnplan